The **Hard** Facts About **Soft** Skills

Coaching Skills for Leaders Who Aren't Afraid to Be 'Soft'

By

Dee Hutchinson

ISBN: 978-1-78808-609-7

You can find out more about Dee and talk to her directly, just join any one of her social media pages.

Join the Dee is for Digital community at
https://www.members.deehutchinson.com

Follow Dee on Facebook at
https://www.facebook.com/iamdeehutchinson

Follow Dee on LinkedIn at
https://www.linkedin.com/in/deehutchinson

Author: Dee Hutchinson

Title: The Hard Facts About Soft Skills

Subtitle: Coaching Skills for Leaders Who Aren't Afraid to Be Soft

Subjects: Leadership; Coaching; Learning & Development; Employee Engagement; Training; Business; Performance Management

Disclaimer:

The material in this publication is of the nature of general comment only, and does not represent professional advice. It is not intended to provide specific guidance for particular circumstances, and it should not be relied upon as the basis for any decision to take action or not take action on any matter that it covers. Readers should obtain professional advice where appropriate, before making any such decision. To the maximum extent permitted by law, the author and publisher disclaim all responsibility and liability to any person, arising directly or indirectly from any person taking action or not taking action based on the information in this publication.

What you will get from this book

A business is much like a growing plant. Despite their obvious differences, both require patience and care so that they can flourish. A vibrant plant requires seeds, soil, water and sunlight in the same way a business needs a skilled manager to nurture talented employees. And with the proper attention to detail, the right manager can make his or her employees bloom just like the healthiest of plants.

In *The Hard Facts About Soft Skills*, author Dee Hutchinson lays out the perfect battle plan for managers who want to succeed. But contrary to the assumption that hard skills are the alpha and omega of employee talent, Hutchinson lays out in detail the importance of soft skills and how managers can effectively harness them to improve their bottom line.

Soft skills—such as a strong work ethic, time-management skills and self-confidence—work hand-in hand with hard skills. It's not enough for your employees to merely possess the latter. Soft skills, which cannot be copied by your competitors, ensure that an already talented employee can maximize their potential and make your company more successful. And such an employee can only become great by a manager who knows how to elevate their potential.

Hutchinson presents her case in a compelling fashion by showing managers how, when and why to coach employees on their team. Communication preferences and coaching best practices are only some of the topics she covers. She details the specific processes managers can use to build rapport with their employees, including the famous GROW coaching model, and she also includes ten useful career coaching tools and templates. As an added bonus, customers who purchase this book will receive access to an online coaching course valued at almost $500.

If you find your employees are not living up to their true potential, *The Hard Facts About Soft Skills* is the book you've been waiting for. No longer will your company fall behind your competitors as your bottom line suffers. With this thorough and easy-to-follow book, you will learn how to communicate with and coach your employees to true success. And as you absorb these new leadership skills, your employees will gladly follow you up the hill on your organization's glorious path to victory.

Contents

About the Author

Dee Hutchinson is the Founder and CEO of Dee is for Digital, a digital learning and development company. Dee has over 20 years of corporate experience and has won over 30 industry awards in the fields of customer experience, employee engagement, and learning & development. She works across the globe with major multi-nationals enabling them to deliver exceptional levels of employee engagement through the deployment of coaching and leadership development programs.

Dee is one of those exceedingly rare finds. Super smart at her job, capable of working at all levels, confident under big pressure, always delivers and is a driving force for positive change in any organization. Dee's ability to make the impossible possible by coaching and motivating the people around her is one of the best I've seen. She was a massive help to me personally and is a key reason for our success. Hoping that one day I get to work with her again.

Marc Norris, Entrepreneur – Investor – Experienced Telco Executive

I have a simple definition of leadership: those qualities that are demonstrated in an adapting situation that enables ordinary people to achieve extraordinary results. If we were to quantify these qualities, it is very evident that Dee possesses them by the bucketful. It's not a term that I have used before on LinkedIn, but her people absolutely LOVE her—and I can understand why. Brimming with initiative, immensely generous with her time, and a drive that inspires success, Dee is fantastic company. If you seek to understand what being in the company of a great leader feels like—one simple fix—spend some time with her!

Mark McCoy MSc MCIPD FLM – Head of HR

Deirdre (Dee) is by far the best people leader I have met in my career to date. Dee has an amazing ability to connect with people and harness what they have to get them to express the best of themselves and, therefore, the best for the customers that they serve. In her core environment of contact centers and customer service, it's an extremely powerful chemical mix, and this is shown in her success so far. However, the mix becomes much more potent when Dee is able to establish key strategic brands for programs of excellence and customer experience that provide purpose, drive and success in any organization. She is a relationship guru of the highest order.

Asim Mirza, Customer Experience & Operations Executive

There are few people in this world that I would rather work with than Dee Hutchinson. Not only is she an excellent executive in the traditional sense—with a keen sense of how to manage, how to operate, and how to be the face of a company, but she is a wonderful human being who also understands the nuances of human behavior in business. Her employees love her for a reason—as do her clients – as do her vendors. She gets business—and she gets people. And she is a great person herself!

Paul Greenberg, Owner The 56 Group LLC

Acknowledgments

For Maurizio, who has always known
the right question to ask.

Grazie.

Ti amo.

Part 1: Introduction

More Questions than Answers

"QUALITY QUESTIONS CREATE A QUALITY LIFE. SUCCESSFUL PEOPLE ASK BETTER QUESTIONS, AND AS A RESULT, THEY GET BETTER ANSWERS."

Tony Robbins

You would think to have more questions than answers would be a bad thing, but that is not true in coaching. And one of my goals for you is that you will finish this book with more questions than answers. You see, one sign of a great coach is they have a tool bag of powerful questions that they can access whenever they need. Questions that, when asked, cause you to pause and reflect. For me, a great question is one that I haven't been asked before, and when probed with such a question, it stops me dead in my tracks. I must take some time to find the answer, and more often than not, if it's a brilliant question, I won't have a response . . . at least not straight away.

The best questions help a light go off in the dark. Not necessarily 'dark' in a bad way but somewhere that we have not shed any light before, or at least not for a long time. And when that light goes off, it opens the door for reflection, insight, change, and action. A great question makes you think. A great question ignites curiosity. A great question leads you to learn something new about yourself.

Take a moment to ask yourself some of these great questions:

1. When it's all said and done, will you have said more than you have done?
2. If the average human lifespan were 40 years, how would you live your life differently?

3. If you could offer a new-born child just one piece of advice, what would it be? And why?
4. What's something you know you do differently than most people?
5. What is the one thing you have not yet done that you want to do? What's holding you back?
6. Are you holding onto something you know you should let go of?
7. Why are you, you?
8. What are you most grateful for?
9. If not now, then when?
10. What would you do differently if you knew nobody would judge you?

I love observing the coaching process in action—it starts with asking one of my coachees a powerful question and then watching their internal processes kick into high gear. Their eyes move around as if they are searching internally for an answer. Or a wry smile comes to their face as if to say, "Now why did you go and ask me that?!" And I sit and wait for the searching to end and the answer to come because the answer always comes. One of the greatest joys of being a coach is that every day it reaffirms in me a belief that I have held for some time now:

We already know all of our answers.

Those answers may not be obvious at the outset, and you may even think you don't know the answers to your questions, but you do. And that is the best way I can describe what a great coach does. They ask you powerful questions that help shine a light on a part of you that was hidden from view or on an answer that had been just out of reach. By shining that light, you discover solutions, insights, and aspects of yourself that lead you towards personal development, change and growth.

As I write this introduction, I am on a Thai Airways flight to Bangkok, and I have been reflecting on some coaching that I conducted in Australia, with some amazing individuals. I have seen a transformation in these people that is astounding and that after no more than two coaching sessions.

I am flying back to Bangkok inspired.

When I hear people say that change is difficult and that most people resist it, I have to say that is not my experience at all. I have witnessed people change right before my eyes. I have experienced people find answers they have long searched for and with just one powerful question. I have seen teams led by inspiring leaders that embrace change like an old friend. I also do not believe that transformational change has to take a long time—months or years. In Australia, I have just witnessed people change, willingly change and transform in the space of hours.

My job as their coach is one and only one. Ask them great questions and then give them the space to find their answers—because they will, and they do—every time. This is one of the many skills that you will learn in this book.

My obsession with questions has been with me for as long as I can remember. I have no idea when it started, but I think it comes from always having been curious about people, wanting to know what makes them tick, what rocks their world, their dreams and aspirations, their fears and concerns, their hopes and loves.

During my research for this book, I wanted to uncover the most difficult or challenging question for someone to answer. I had assumed it would probably be one of those philosophical questions like "Why am I here?" or "What is my purpose?" or "What do I want my legacy to be?" etc. I couldn't find a definitive answer, so I looked to my coaching for inspiration. I have coached thousands of people, and the one question I have found that consistently stops people in their tracks is "What do you want?"

A deceptively simple question, yet the one that my coachees find the most difficult to answer.

Go ahead. Try it right now. Ask yourself, "What do I want?" More specifically, "What do I want from my life?" Do you have a clear and detailed answer to that question? If your answer is short like "I want to be happy," which is a lovely response but not nearly precise enough for me, we would need to continue asking questions like:

- What does happy mean to you?
- On a scale of one to ten, how happy are you right now?
- What would it take to get you to a ten?
- How will you know when you are totally happy?
- What will be different then as compared to now?
- What have you already done to achieve total happiness?
- What is preventing you from being totally happy right now?

This week in Australia, one of my coachees was unable to answer the "What do you want?" question, and he got quite frustrated with himself during the coaching session . . . how could he not know the answer to such a simple question? He tossed and turned that night, and when he came to see me the next day, he had already found his answer—what he wanted and much, much more (despite having told me innumerable times during the coaching session that he did not have any idea what he wanted from his life).

I witnessed this person transform so monumentally. He told me what he wanted, his mission, and all the ways he now feels differently about himself and his capabilities.

A light had gone off and is now shining brightly.

This nicely brings me to the title of my book *The Hard Facts About Soft Skills*. For a long time now, I have wanted to shine a light on something I have struggled with for quite a while, and it has been the primary motivation for me to write this book.

Let me tell you a story.

I remember the very first time I was asked by a manager, "Do you feel you are too close to your team?" (A very leading question, don't you think?) I was working for a major multi-national in Dublin, Ireland, and I was in my very first team leader role. I didn't think I was too close to my team (what does too close mean anyway?), but I knew that because he'd asked the question, he thought I was. That was the very first time I realized that being observed as being "too close" with my team members was not necessarily viewed as a positive thing. It was also the first time I realized the power that feedback from a manager could have on an employee—both positive and negative. So much so, I haven't forgotten that conversation, and it has held a lot of power over me for quite a long time.

The funny thing is, right before he asked me that question, I had just had a conversation with one of my team who was thinking of leaving, and I had managed to convince her to change her mind. In that 30-minute conversation, I had saved the company anywhere between €6,000 and €9,000 in replacement costs. Back then, she would have been on an annual salary of €12,000 as a call center agent, and the latest statistics from SHRM predict that every time a business replaces a salaried employee, it costs anywhere between 6 to 9 months' salary. But that didn't, and still doesn't seem to matter to most companies because it is not tangible or hard enough. It doesn't show on the books, so it doesn't count! An invisible intangible, yet tangible benefit.

I knew that by showing a genuine interest in my team, by spending as much time with them as I could, by being available to them whenever they needed would only serve to build a phenomenal team, AND that would give us a better chance of consistently delivering outstanding results. Which we did, by the way. A team where trust was at our core. Where my team members could talk to me about leaving the company and not worry that I would judge, criticize, or get angry.

That was the first, but certainly not the last time that I would be asked similar questions or hear subtle and uncomplimentary comments about my leadership style. I wouldn't have minded if my teams were not performing, but they were performing and then some. My teams have won awards and been recognized internationally for their achievements, which have always reflected well on them and the company overall. However, my leadership style has more often than not been referred to as "touchy-feely" and wait for it, "warm and fuzzy!"

I could seriously use some choice words every time I hear those descriptions, but it is a realistic reflection of how an "employee-oriented" (that would be my preferred term) style of leadership is perceived in many organizations. And I'm tired of it! Sick of it, to be honest.

More than twenty years forward from that first conversation in Dublin, older and wiser, I don't see any great change in the value companies put on the development of their leaders' soft skills or the positive impact of those leaders who use their soft skills to build highly engaged and effective teams. In fact, in 2014, Deloitte Consulting published a report on global workforce trends and looked at the gaps between what the workforce needs and what companies are capable of providing. The biggest gap identified is unsurprisingly in the area of leadership development.

In the short and near term, around the world and in every industry vertical, the lack of qualified leadership and leadership training has been identified as the number one issue facing enterprises of all sizes. It is a major problem for the corporate world.

And what isn't surprising here, as I look back over the years since I started my career, is that there has been little to no change in the sphere of leadership learning and development, and I would say little to no change in the approach to people management either. When you compare this to the evolution, even revolution in technology, strategy, product development, marketing—even customer experience—I can think of multiple examples of how these areas of business have totally evolved in their structure, thinking, processes, user focus, etc. When it comes to development and people management, I just do not see anywhere near the same pace of transformative change.

It is a given that humans do not change at the same pace as technology, that's for sure. But I would still expect some evolution when it comes to the most valuable assets that any organization can possess—their human capital. And before you say it, yes, we have experienced the introduction of online training or e-learning, but I see this more often deployed as a cost-saving initiative rather than a powerful, engaging platform to actively develop and enhance specific skills, particularly for the leadership audience.

To be honest, how I have been managed as an employee from 20 years ago right up to very recently has not changed at all. At times, I have been lucky to work for some amazing managers, "lucky" being the operative word. I don't understand why in this day and age an employee has to "be lucky" to get a leader who inspires them, develops them, challenges them, engages them, and so on. And if I look at it in terms of numbers (and I actually calculated this), when I count up all the people I have reported to throughout my career, only 20% of those managers would fall in the "amazing leader" category. Fifty percent would fall in the "average" category and 30% in the "I wouldn't wish them on my worst enemy" category.

If you were to take a similar look at your "manager history," what would your numbers look like? And how about right now, how are YOU doing as a leader, and how is your leader managing you?

Given that the primary subject of this book is about questions, why not ask yourself these questions?

1. When was the last time you received <u>meaningful</u> feedback from your manager?

2. When was the last time you gave meaningful feedback to one of your team?
3. When was the last time you were recognized or rewarded for the work you do?
4. When was the last time you rewarded or recognized a member of your team?
5. Do you feel that your company genuinely cares about your career?
6. Do your team members know that you genuinely care about their careers?
7. On a scale of 1 to 10, how satisfied are you with your development?
8. How do you think your team would rate their satisfaction with their development?

As you will read later in this book, I believe that there is a solution to every problem, and despite the many challenges I see facing the development of today's and tomorrow's leaders, I also do believe this presents an incredible opportunity for those willing to embrace it. So, let's take a moment to look at some of those opportunities.

OPPORTUNITY 1: SOFT SKILLS ARE GOOD FOR BUSINESS

In reality, there is nothing "warm and fuzzy" about soft skills or the leaders who deploy them to great effect. Let me share a few cold, hard facts with you:

1. According to the Gallup organization, building engaged, high-performance teams not only reduces absenteeism, employee turnover, and workplace accidents, it also increases productivity and profitability—by more than 20 percent.
2. Engaged teams create an exponential lift in profitability. Aon Hewitt, for example, found that in a $5B organization, a one percent improvement in engagement increased profitability by $20M. Five percent improvement resulted in gains of $102M profitability, and 10 percent improvement resulted in $204M profitability.
3. According to Gallup's research, companies with engaged workforces have higher earnings per share (EPS), and they seem to have recovered

> from the recession at a faster rate. Companies with an average of 9.3 engaged employees for every actively disengaged employee in 2010–2011 experienced 147% higher EPS compared with their competition in 2011–2012. Companies with an average of 2.6 engaged employees for every actively disengaged employee, in contrast, experienced 2% lower EPS compared with their competition during that same time period.

I can tell you right now that leaders who have highly engaged teams have achieved this goal primarily through the deployment of their soft skills, not their hard ones. I don't believe the benefits outlined above could ever or should ever be described as SOFT even though the skill set required to lead highly engaged employees and teams are described as such.

My "soft" leadership style has been fundamental in the management of critical strategic projects including increasing Employee Net Promoter Score (ENPS) from -53 to +12 in less than nine months for a telecommunications business. I can assure you that when it comes to employee engagement, you cannot just tell people to "get engaged or else." It hasn't been my hard skills (although they do play a part) that have enabled me to get the results that I have. It has been primarily my ability to quickly build trust with people, communicate effectively and meaningfully, influence and cajole where necessary, motivate and inspire, be believable and authentic, and described as a person "who genuinely cares about employees' well-being."

One of the biggest disappointments for today's leaders and the leaders we should be developing for the future is that they are not being taught or coached in the type of skills that I describe above. In fact, many of these skills cannot be learned in a classroom. They are developed over time. I learned these skills myself over the space of years—many from brilliant leaders and sometimes from not-so-great leaders who taught me how not to do things (equally valuable lessons). Organizations need to be far better equipped to enable our leaders to develop the skills they need to operate at the highest levels, particularly when the skills that will help differentiate them the most and make the biggest impact for their organizations and their employees are indeed "soft."

Consider for a moment that the strongest driver of employee engagement is a **sense of feeling valued and involved**, and this can be broken down into several components:

1. Involvement in decision making
2. Ability to voice ideas and have managers who listen to these views and value their employees' contributions
3. Ample opportunities for career development and progression
4. The belief that the company is genuinely concerned about employees' health and well-being.

The line manager clearly has a very important role in fostering an employee's sense of involvement and feeling valued. I would argue that the line manager is the single most important person to positively (or negatively) impact how engaged an employee feels about the company they work for.

So, for organizations to experience the benefit of 20% increases in productivity and profitability or higher earnings per share, it is in their interests to equip their leaders with the necessary skills to ensure the highest levels of employee engagement in their teams. The most effective way to achieve this is to teach leaders how to coach.

I can guarantee that of all of the skills we could teach our leaders, coaching skills will have the greatest impact on performance, productivity, motivation, and engagement. It is a skill that will never go out of fashion and over the long term will serve the manager immensely in becoming a highly effective senior leader who can easily balance an employee-centered leadership style with a clinical focus on high performance and achieving goals.

I don't know an organization in the world that does not want to become more productive or profitable . . . do you? Yet far too many are not seizing the opportunities open to them through the application of coaching principles. If you currently work for an organization like this, I have one coaching question for you . . .

What is stopping you?

OPPORTUNITY 2:
WATCH YOUR LANGUAGE

I believe that the words we use are important and they are embedded with a lot of meaning. I have always been curious about language, and after years of study, I can quite accurately pinpoint a person's personality traits and preferences based on the words they use to communicate with me.

I also think the fact that some extremely useful behaviors/competencies/characteristics—whatever you want to call them—have been defined as "soft," and have led to them being, at best, devalued and, at worst, completely ignored.

The words we choose to describe concepts and strategies have plenty of embedded meaning, and the fact that someone chooses to represent an entire set of skills as "soft" is not lost on me. When you Google the definition of "soft," this is the first result you get back:

adjective

1. *Easy to mould, cut, compress, or fold; not hard or firm to the touch "soft margarine"*

   synonyms: mushy, squashy, pulpy, pappy, slushy, sloppy, squelchy, squishy, oozy, doughy, semi-liquid

2. *Having a pleasing quality involving a subtle effect or contrast rather than sharp definition.*
   "the soft glow of the lamps"

   synonyms: dim, low, faint, shaded, muted, mellow

adverb

1. *In a quiet or gentle way*

   "I can just speak soft and she'll hear me."

2. *Informal*

   In a weak or foolish way
   "don't talk soft"

I don't think I need to point out that there is nothing in those descriptions that would lead you to believe that anything or anyone being described in "soft" terms is a good thing! But, hold on. It gets worse. Just take a look at some of the most common ways the word "soft" is used in the English language:

Soft Sell

To have a soft touch

To have a soft spot for something/someone

To be soft on something/someone

And my personal favorite . . .

To be soft in the head

Now look at this definition of hard skills:

Specific, teachable abilities that can be defined and measured, such as typing, writing, math, reading and the ability to use software programs. By contrast, soft skills are less tangible and harder to quantify, such as etiquette, getting along with others, listening and engaging in small talk.

"Listening and engaging in small talk?" No wonder soft skills aren't taken seriously. We need to make some drastic changes in the language that we use to describe some of the most powerful skills a leader can possess, and we need to make them now.

What I would like to suggest is, that from today, we no longer use the term "soft skills," but we use the phrase "standout skills" instead, because when these skills are deployed by leaders, their employees, and their organizations, the results are that they "stand out" (for all the right reasons) when compared to their competitors. The facts already prove it. Just by changing the wording, it gives the phrase what I can only describe as a distinctive energy.

Would you prefer to go to soft skills training or to training that will help you stand out in your current role? I know what my answer is. Do CEOs want to invest budget in developing employees' emotional intelligence, or would they prefer to develop skill sets that ensure the organization stands out for their levels of performance, productivity, and employee engagement?

I say we start to stand up for standout skills!

In my opinion, the use of this kind of language is just a symptom of a larger problem. I have interviewed many CEOs as part of my research for this book. I wanted to get a better understanding of why a senior executive would look unfavorably at someone who demonstrates an employee-centered style of leadership and the "standout" skills that come with it. The two most common explanations I was given are:

1. An employee-centered style of leadership can be considered a "slower" way of achieving results when compared to leaders who take a more "task-oriented" approach.
2. In some cases, an employee-centered approach can be seen as "getting in the way" of achieving results.

With that kind of mindset, it kind of makes sense why we would refer to certain skills as "soft." The words "soft" and "results" rarely, if ever, come up in the same sentence, do they? I'm shaking my head as I reread this because it is shocking to me that an organization could think this way; however, with my coaching hat on, I do know that:

1. There are reasons for this thinking and probably good reasons, too.
2. We need to understand the problem before we can create a better solution.
3. We need to understand the fears, worries, and pressures facing our key decision makers.
4. We need to make it easy for executives to choose coaching as a solution not just to employee engagement but also to achievement of business goals.

I have made sure to include plenty of "facts" in this book so that you can share them with your senior leadership team. As coaches and leaders, we need to take some ownership in how we communicate and the language we use to explain the benefits of coaching to our organizations. And we also need to become responsible for educating those same executives as to what coaching is and is not; what it can help achieve; that it is not a "slow" process but can produce immediate results; and much more.

In my own experience, my teams and I have achieved amazing results, not despite my leadership style but precisely because of my leadership style. The facts demonstrate over and over again that highly engaged teams led by leaders who can coach produce better results every single time. It is our "standout" skills that differentiate us in a positive, competitive, and high-performing way. We "stand out" because of our skills, not in spite of them.

OPPORTUNITY 3: TAKE A HOLISTIC VIEW OF LEARNING & DEVELOPMENT

Let's start to take a more holistic view of the skills, behaviors, and competencies that successful leaders possess. Our leaders' performance is based on a mixture of all their experiences, skills, knowledge, personality, upbringing, education, values, and so on. To only talk about their "skills" is ignoring all the other valuable and important components that make them who they are—unique.

I have repeatedly seen expensive learning development programs rolled out across organizations that have been abject failures when it comes to actually raising the performance of their target audience. At first glance, they seem to have everything covered: a defined target audience, clear learning outcomes, multiple channels for delivery, experienced trainers, input from the students, assessment processes, feedback mechanisms, etc., but they still have not tangibly improved the leaders' or company's performance. Why?

Let me start by giving you a simple example for illustration purposes.

Sample Learning Outcome

Teach mid-level leaders to be able to prepare and present effective presentations to the senior management team.

Now, there is a mixture of hard and soft skills that could be covered in a training course of this kind:

1. How to use Microsoft PowerPoint—hard skill
2. How to research your presentation topic—hard skill
3. How to construct your presentation—hard skill
4. Know your audience—soft skill
5. Set-up of the presentation room—hard skill
6. Use of handouts and notes—hard skill
7. How to present in an engaging manner—soft skill
8. How to handle questions—soft skill

The course would probably also include some time to practice their presentation skills to get feedback from the class. Good idea, right? But something is missing.

Is it possible for a leader to attend a course of this kind, pass the exam with flying colors, and still not be a good presenter? The answer to that is an absolute yes, and I see it all the time. So, what have we missed out on? For me, we have neglected the individual—more precisely, the underlying characteristics that a person has when they can present at the highest levels (e.g., confidence, self-esteem, an ability to handle pressure, a good sense of humor). Even though some of these topics could be covered in a classroom training, the likelihood is that they won't be. Why not?

Well, in the example of a presentation skills or public speaking skills training:

1. The training is not designed to identify and/or address limiting beliefs you have about your presenting skills; e.g., *I don't want to look bad in front of senior management or I'm afraid I will make a mistake and look silly.*
2. The ability to present well is often contextual; e.g., students are comfortable presenting in front of other students who are their peers but fall apart when the audience is more senior.
3. When presenting during the course, if a student shows signs of nervousness, they will be told to keep practicing and they will get

better. Sometimes this is the case; however, that is a pretty painful way to learn and can cause damage to the individual's reputation and career prospects.

4. Confidence is a skill that is grown and developed over time, not just learned in a one-day classroom training. The same can be said of qualities like resilience, flexibility, courage, determination, problem-solving, patience, and the list goes on and on.

The truth of the matter is we have been letting down our leaders for quite a long time, so it stands to reason that the Deloitte report identifies Leadership Development as being an area that requires urgent attention.

We have not been taking a holistic view of our leaders' needs and requirements. We have just been looking at the hard, and to a lesser extent, the standout skills, and missing a whole big chunk of behaviors and attributes that underpin how successfully an individual can deploy their hard and standout skill sets. I have had conversations with companies whose senior executives were not performing despite being given the best training available, and despite seeming, at face value, to have all the skills (both hard and standout) necessary to do their jobs well. But looking at face value is just not close enough. It's part of the problem. No one in an interview is going to mention that they may have a fear of failure, and more than likely, they may be entirely unaware of it themselves. Their boss may not be able to identify a fear of failure, but they do see behaviors like indecisiveness, so they send the individual on a decision-making course that—you guessed it—does not solve their problem at all.

What I'm getting to is another FACT of leadership development that requires us to look for what cannot be seen, even by the leader (or the individual) themselves. The underlying beliefs, values, and behaviors that lie below the water (taking the iceberg analogy). We must train our leaders to identify these issues and provide coaching to help them develop further. We need to help our leaders shine a light on the areas of their performance that they may have a "blind spot" to.

You cannot have a truly successful leadership program without incorporating an element of one-on-one coaching, and the more senior the leader, the higher the proportion of coaching should be.

When the likes of Bill Gates (founder of Microsoft) and Eric Schmidt (Chairman of Google) say, "Everyone needs a coach," including themselves, then there must be something to it. According to Bill Gates, "We all need people to give us feedback. That's how we improve." And Schmidt says, "The one thing that people are never good at is seeing themselves as people see them," and thus one of the main benefits of having a coach is to give the individual a different perspective.

Let's take another example:

This time we'll go for a skill set that many research papers are saying is highly desirable for a CEO, and that is "Business Acumen." Raymond R. Reilly of the Ross School of Business at the University of Michigan and Gregory P. Reilly of the University of Connecticut document traits that individuals with business acumen possess:

- An acute perception of the dimensions of business issues
- Ability to make sense out of complexity and an uncertain future
- Cognizance of the implications of a choice for all the affected parties
- Decisiveness
- Flexibility for further change if warranted in the future.

Now in a training program for developing CEO business acumen, we would likely discuss the business issues facing the company and probably have some exercises that allow the learners to brainstorm, dimension, and solve real business problems. We may also look at examples of business problems and how they were solved by other companies—some sample case studies or best practices. It starts to get interesting when making sense of complexity and an uncertain future—necessary because there isn't a leader in the world who shouldn't be concerned about this. The training could show you how to break down complex problems with some creative problem-solving theory, but what if the learner has limiting beliefs around change and uncertainty—a very common fear for the majority of the world's population. How would fear of change or uncertainty show up in someone's behavior that could impact their performance on the job?

I have personally seen leaders who are uncomfortable with change unconsciously reacting to it by exerting extra effort and control in keeping things the same, e.g., deciding not to make some simple decisions to improve how something is done and instead preferring to maintain the status quo. I have seen these same leaders require and request an inordinate amount of information and data before feeling comfortable enough to make a decision. They required an increased amount of certainty before moving forward which in many cases considerably delayed decision-making and taking action. And strangely enough, decisiveness is also a key attribute when it comes to business acumen.

Without an experienced coach, the leader may not recognize their resistance to change. We all have our blind spots. A straightforward and effective coaching session could bring this to the CEO's attention, and the coach could then enable the leader to take the steps necessary to address any other concerns they may have. The beauty of this approach is that now the CEO becomes aware of this limiting belief or behavior and will be better able to address it the next time it shows up. This type of developmental requirement would rarely—if ever—be picked up in a training scenario unless the trainer had extensive coaching experience.

For our leaders to reach their fullest potential, they must be led by leaders who can and want to coach. We must be able to shine a light on an individual's limiting beliefs (those beliefs about themselves and their capabilities that hold them back) because it is your job as an employee-centered leader to remove roadblocks to their success however these barriers present themselves. The power of coaching partnered with taking a holistic approach to learning and development is a recipe for success—success for the employee, the leader, the organization and its shareholders.

OPPORTUNITY 4:
BRILLIANT BASICS

To be clear, what I am asking is for us to get the basics of people management right and execute those same basics brilliantly and consistently—brilliant leadership basics. The biggest transformation that we could make in this area is to make brilliant basics non-negotiable—where we are no longer having conversations about how important emotional intelligence is or if high employee engagement leads to higher revenues. It is a given that a brilliant basics approach to leadership is the de facto way of leading for any serious organization, and nothing less than that is tolerated.

In order to achieve this, we would start by recognizing that "vanilla version" leadership training has become redundant, with a move to more personalized and targeted development unique to the leader in question. And this targeted approach is frequent, in real time and ongoing, not just a one-day class or off-site intervention. All people managers are taught coaching skills as part of their on-boarding, and they receive ongoing coaching development to hone their skills. Coaching is no longer a distinct, stand-alone activity but is fully integrated into how a leader operates, communicates, and motivates. Their standout skills result in standout performance, problem-solving, and innovation.

We would start our brilliant leadership basics by being clear on exactly what the basics are (and they will most probably differ by organization). We need to ask the questions: What are the basics skills needed for a brilliant leader, and more specifically, what are the skills our leaders need to achieve the highest levels of employee engagement? Because we know that with high employee engagement comes standout business results. The following graphic displays the Maslow Hierarchy of Needs applied to employee engagement, and it brilliantly illustrates how an employee feels at each level of the hierarchy.

At the bottom of the pyramid are those employees in the 'Survival' level and who are totally disengaged. A person at this level of the hierarchy would say things like "I'm only here for the money" or "I'm leaving as soon as I can" or 'My work doesn't excite me." They are obviously demotivated and just buying time until they can leave that organization.

Then we move up one level to 'Security' and here we find employees who are not engaged but not yet totally disengaged. They are slightly less demotivated than at the 'Survival' level and complain about things like not liking their manager, having poor working conditions, they have more sick days than normal and are not interested in doing overtime when requested. They are also highly likely to be actively job hunting.

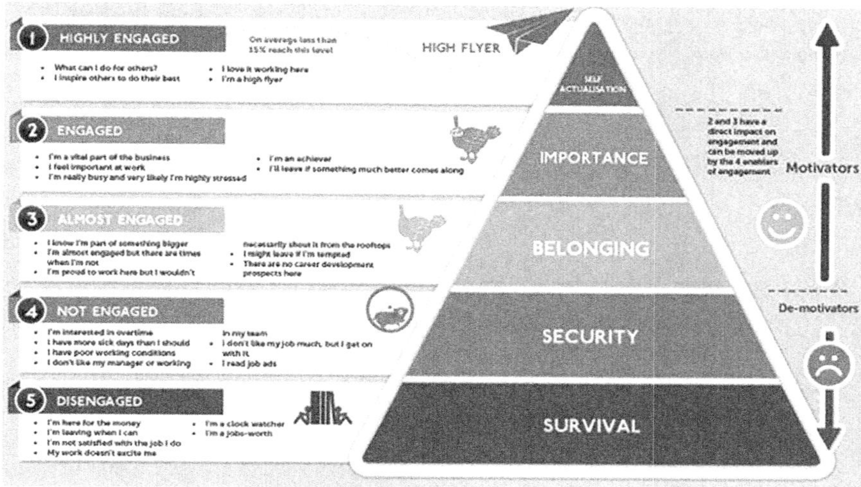

As we move up the hierarchy, we get to employees who feel 'Belonging'—they are 'almost engaged' but not totally engaged yet. They are in the Belonging level because they do feel that they are part of something and in many cases are proud to work for their company, but they won't necessarily shout it from the rooftops. They have less to complain about than the people in the lower two levels and their concerns will relate specifically to lack of learning and career development opportunities.

Now we get to employees who are engaged, and who reside in the 'Importance' level precisely because they feel like they are an important part of the organization. They feel valued, they know they are contributing to the success of the business. This employee would tend to be a high achiever, always busy and likely to be stressed. And despite being engaged they may consider leaving but only if something much better came along.

And last but not least, the highly-engaged employees—the 'highflyers' who are at the top of the pyramid in 'Self Actualization.' On average less than fifteen percent of all employees will sit at this level. They are characterized as loving their jobs and are role models for others. They think less about their own needs because they are already achieving everything they want and are in the position to consider how they can help and inspire others.

In the context of Brilliant Basics and achieving the highest possible levels of employee engagement, an organization and its leaders can easily recognize and measure the symptoms and behaviors of employees at the lower levels of the hierarchy because they are in tune with how those individuals may behave, speak and act. They are also clear on how to move people up through the hierarchy out of disengagement and towards high engagement.

For me, the top ten skills that any leader would require to lead people to the highest levels of engagement and model brilliant leadership basics are:

1. The ability to build trust
2. Knowing how to make people feel safe
3. Communicating with passion, authenticity, and honesty
4. Setting clear goals and planning to overachieve
5. Giving consistent, meaningful, and honest feedback
6. Coaching for high performance and potential
7. Motivating and celebrating success
8. Rewarding and recognizing high performance
9. Modeling inspiration in the workplace
10. Knowing your stuff and keeping your skills sharp.

With the exception of "Knowing your stuff," the remaining nine skills would be considered standout skills, and all of these skills can be learned through coaching training. In order to be a highly effective coach, you must be able to build trust, make people feel safe, communicate superbly, set goals, give feedback, motivate, etc., so everything you require to be the best leader you can be is totally aligned to being a great coach (and covered in this book).

OPPORTUNITY 5:
70-20-10

70-20-10 is a commonly used model for learning and development used within the training profession. It describes the optimal sources of learning by successful managers, and it holds that individuals obtain 70% of their knowledge from on-the-job experiences, 20% from their interactions with others, and 10% from formal educational events, e.g., classroom and online training.

The model was created in the 1980s by three researchers and authors working with the Center for Creative Leadership, a non-profit educational institution in Greensboro, N.C. The three—Morgan McCall, Michael M. Lombardo, and Robert A. Eichinger—were researching the key developmental experiences of successful managers.

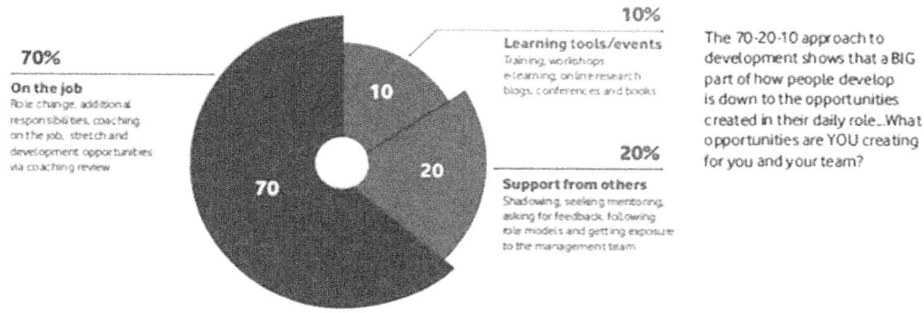

Ref. Centre for Creative Leadership

I want to bring this model to your attention as it is widely used in many organizations and can be somewhat unpopular with employees as they view it as a means for the company to be 'cheap' with their training. The reality is that very few professionals view on-the-job training and support from others as adequate or valuable forms of learning or development.

I have felt that way about this model, yet I also agree that the most powerful learning experiences I have had have been on-the-job through experiential learning, but something is missing from this model.

I think this model requires some documented assumptions to underpin its efficacy. The kinds of questions that come to mind when I look at this model are:

- What if the manager doesn't know how to coach his/her team on the job?
- What if the manager doesn't want/like/value coaching his/her team?
- What if no stretch or developmental opportunities are open to the employee?
- What if there are no effective feedback mechanisms in place?
- What if on-the-job development/feedback/coaching are not measured or managed?

- What if there are no opportunities to shadow or get mentoring from more senior colleagues?
- What if it's considered normal to be in the same job for more than three years, and opportunities for promotion are few?

Do you see where I am going with this? In my opinion, the 70-20-10 model presumes an ideal scenario where the employee has a manager who is actively engaged in their development; where the same manager has been developed themselves to understand, apply, and develop their own skills; where the organization values, measures, and monitors coaching, effective feedback, and an employee's ongoing development or lack of.

Plus, shouldn't the model be adapted for different contexts? For example, a newly recruited employee may require a higher percentage of training for their first 6 months in the role. An employee who has been in the job for more than 3 years and now can do their job blindfolded may require more support from others and learning events to keep them engaged and developing for future roles.

As much as I am a supporter of on-the-job and experiential learning, as Alfred E. Neuman said, "The problem with learning from experience is that you always get the test before the lesson." This is a great way of learning for some, but not for all. And an organization that truly allows for learning by making mistakes on the job must also have a culture and leaders that do not punish mistakes. This requires a very different approach to leadership, and one that I rarely see in most organizations.

And what does all of this have to do with coaching? Well, if you use the 70-20-10 model in your organization and if you want to make the most from this model, then you must have leaders who can and will coach their teams. To truly make the most of on-the-job learning and development through support from others, leaders must have the required skill sets to do this effectively.

This means that every leader in the business has been trained as a coach and receives ongoing development to grow and enhance their coaching abilities. This must take place from the top of the organization down because all leaders, no matter their seniority, benefit from coaching.

I believe that an organization that takes this approach will:

- Reduce spending on ineffective training programs
- Increase employee engagement
- Increase productivity
- Reduce the length of learning curves
- Improve problem-solving (time and quality)
- Increase creativity, innovation and solution-oriented thinking.

OPPORTUNITY 6: LEARNING CULTURE RATHER THAN COACHING CULTURE

I don't particularly like the term "coaching culture," and with my corporate hat on, I don't like being advised to have a coaching culture that is a bit messed up given that I am a coach, right? The reason I resist the coaching culture approach is I would prefer businesses to talk about having a learning culture instead, of which coaching is a big part of that overall strategy.

Coaching can impact many talent and organizational outcomes, but it is not a solution for every learning and development challenge. Sometimes training is the answer, or mentoring or feedback, all of which differ from coaching (we will cover the precise differences a little later.) However, the inclusion of coaching as part of the overall learning culture does have its benefits.

According to the International Coaching Federation (ICF), "a strong coaching culture positively correlates with employee engagement and financial performance. Nearly two-thirds of respondents from organizations with strong coaching cultures rate their employees as being 'highly engaged,' compared to only half from organizations without strong coaching cultures." Regarding financial impact, "51% of respondents from organizations with strong coaching cultures report their 2015 revenue to be above that of their industry peer group, compared to 38% from all other organizations."

In a study by the Human Capital Institute (HCI) and the International Coach Federation (ICF), of almost 900 human resources (HR), learning and development (L&D), and talent management (TM) professionals, leaders and managers, the key research findings include:

- Improved team performance, increased employee engagement, and increased productivity are the top outcomes of coaching and are reported by more than fifty percent of all survey respondents.
- Lack of time and lack of accountability are the top reported impediments to using coaching skills.
- When compared to prior studies, the percentage of respondents reporting their organizations' use of professional coach practitioners has declined, and the most common approach is for managers/leaders to conduct coaching (up nine percent since 2014).
- The most important coaching competencies identified for leaders are the ability to establish trust, apply ethical standards, and practice active listening skills.
- Coaching skills training for managers is stated as a critical component when building a coaching culture, with sixteen percent of respondents saying their organizations plan to offer leaders coach-specific training from a program that was approved by a professional coaching organization. That said, most managers/leaders receive coaching skills training from their L&D department, HR department, and internal coach practitioners.

Whether you realize it or not, your organization already has a learning culture. If you employ human beings, then learning happens in your workplace every day because we're biologically hardwired to learn. We literally cannot stop ourselves from doing it.

The real question is what type of learning culture do you have? Is it a culture that transforms, develops, and innovates, and is tightly linked to the goals of the business? Or is it a culture that punishes mistakes, stifles creativity, inhibits growth, and depresses talent?

The benefits of having a learning culture are very similar to those identified for high employee engagement:

- High productivity, retention, and customer satisfaction
- Enhanced creativity and innovation
- Improved levels of employee morale and motivation
- Better overall business results

A successful company doesn't merely just provide opportunities for formal training but cultivates a model that creates continuous opportunities for learning. Examples of formalized informal learning would include feedback, coaching, mentoring, and training that can be requested whenever the employee needs it. Just take a look at this image provided by Bersin & Deloitte, 2013:

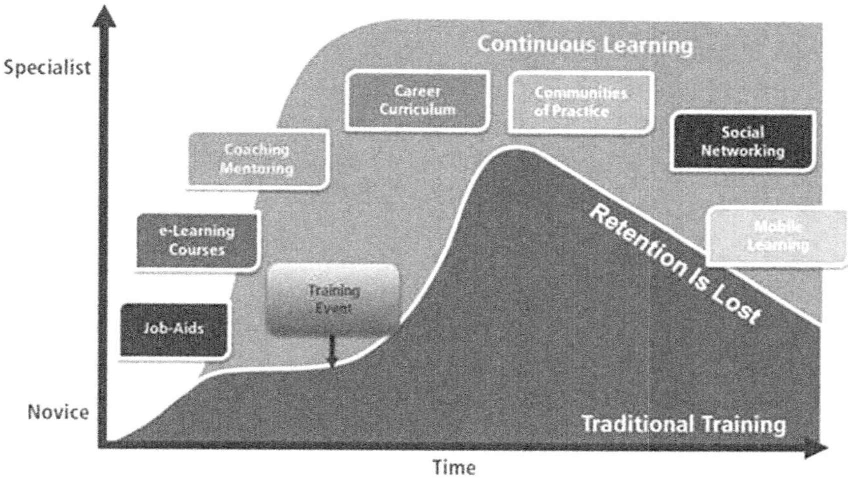

This illustrates that traditional approaches to training, generally one-off training events, result in the knowledge being retained by the employee decreasing over time whereas continuous learning across multiple channels ensures high retention rates over the longer term. This is one of the many reasons why coaching is so effective, particularly when facilitated by the employee's manager:

1. It is continuous
2. It can happen in the moment
3. It is contextual
4. It is personalized.

When coaching is complemented with other forms of development like e-learning, career development, training, performance feedback, and self-study, it becomes a powerful learning engine and one that employees can actively engage with and experience the benefits of.

Conclusions

These are exciting times in the world of coaching and leadership development. There are so many opportunities for you, your team and your organizations to prosper and propel your performance to higher levels. It would seem to be too good to be true, that just coaching, could be a catalyst for this kind of development and growth. However, the facts and evidence available, from multiple sources, show that when workplace coaching is implemented the benefits are tangible, financial, measurable and exponential.

If you and your organization want to stand out then you are absolutely reading the right book to make that happen.

In the upcoming chapters, you will prepare yourself with all the skills necessary to become an exceptional workplace coach.

Part 2:

Before You Start Coaching

Introduction

Welcome to part two of this book and now we can get stuck into the skills you will want to develop to become an exceptional workplace coach. Rather than jumping straight into the GROW model of coaching which we will cover extensively in part three, I wanted first to cover some essential concepts and frameworks that will help you to apply your coaching skills to maximum effect.

First, we will discuss what coaching is and what it is not as well as looking at the differences between coaching, training, mentoring and counseling. These terms are frequently misused, and it is important that you are clear on when and how each method is used. I will introduce you to the Logical Levels of Learning formulated by the anthropologist, Gregory Bateson, a framework which I refer to regularly and that will assist you to confidently choose the most appropriate learning or coaching intervention for your employees.

We will deep dive into one of my favorite coaching topics—limiting beliefs—what are they, how do you identify them, how do they hold you back, how do you get rid of them, etc. Much of my workplace coaching relates to employees' limiting beliefs, so this will be a crucial chapter for you to understand. I have included plenty of exercises, and I encourage you to take the necessary time to complete them thoroughly—these will go a long way to ensure you fully understand the concepts and can apply them to yourself and others.

You will discover, in part three, the importance of being able to create rapport with your coachee and to build said rapport you must become familiar with how we communicate, our communication preferences and the application of sensory acuity. The good news is you already know how to do all of this—you've been communicating since you were a baby, right? These chapters will give you a better appreciation of what is going on behind our communication, why we communicate the way we do, how we can interact move effectively with others to create win-win relationships and how to use verbal and nonverbal body language to powerful effect.

I mentioned at the start of this book that I want to leave you with more questions than answers and the chapter on questions does just that. I have included examples of powerful questions that you can use in multiple scenarios:

- When you want to get to know someone better
- Questions for new members of your team
- How to respond with a question when being asked for advice
- Ice-breaking questions to kick off meetings
- Questions for brainstorming and problem-solving
- Coaching questions to use when someone is procrastinating or making excuses
- The best questions to use to get to know your boss
- Career development and professional growth questions.

There will be nothing stopping you from starting to use these questions straight away and I encourage you to put these into practice as soon as you can! And if that wasn't enough questions there will be more to come when we cover the GROW Model in part three.

Towards the end of this chapter, we will start to focus on specific skills to develop your coaching abilities. I cover eleven coaching guidelines and three beliefs for professional excellence. I have included exercises to develop your self-awareness which you can also use with your coachees and a detailed model for how to design and document coaching goals and outcomes.

What Is Coaching?

So, what is coaching? Well, that's a really good question and one that seems to have more than one answer. Just Google definitions of coaching and you'll find many—one more confusing than the next. I believe this lack of agreement or clarity on what coaching is and is not has damaged its reputation in the corporate world. I have worked with companies that view coaching as a type of therapy for "problematic employees," and this couldn't be further from the truth. Or they view coaching as just a "talking shop" for employees to air grievances and talk about their problems, thus lacking tangible benefits for the company.

The International Coaching Federation defines professional coaching as:

> *Partnering with clients in a thought-provoking and creative process that inspires them to maximize their personal and professional potential.*

I honestly think this description is far too vague, and if I were to read that with my corporate hat on, I would be put off coaching by that description. I prefer to describe workplace coaching as a way of developing employees to improve their effectiveness and performance, and enabling them to achieve their full potential. It is results and action-oriented. The benefits are immediate, measurable, and exponential.

Coaching is just another means to develop an employee in a very personalized way. Through coaching, an employee can unlock their potential, address performance challenges, and remove barriers to their achievements. Let's look at how coaching compares to training, mentoring, and counseling.

Coaching Is Not Training

Training and coaching both promote learning; however, they do so in different ways. Training is about teaching specific skills, whereas coaching is about enabling someone to find solutions themselves and helping them learn on the job. Training tends to happen in a classroom (traditional or virtual) and is a one-off event. Coaching takes place in the office, occurs in real time (when carried out by a manager), and is easily integrated into day-to-day workplace conversations. Training is delivered by an external trainer or someone from the internal training team. Coaching is facilitated by a qualified coach or the individual's manager. The efficacy of training is measured by an exam at the end of the course. The efficacy of coaching is measured by action taken by the coachee and achievement of their goal(s). Training happens in a "one to many" scenario. Coaching occurs in a "one to one" scenario.

Coaching Is Not Mentoring

Although easily confused, coaching and mentoring are not the same. A mentor is someone more senior (in organizational seniority and age) than the individual they mentor. They have extensive experience in their field, and they share this experience with their mentee. They can be from within the organization or not and are chosen by the individual because they are looking to gain developmental help in a specific area. The mentor-mentee relationship is one of elder statesperson with young up-and-comer.

A coach does not have to be more senior than the person being coached, and they don't even have to have work experience within the same field. The coach does not give advice but uses questions and feedback to facilitate learning and development. The coach can be an external coaching practitioner and/or the individual's line manager. The mentor will likely meet their mentee monthly. The manager coaches the individual in real time, as and when necessary.

Coaching Is Not Counseling

Probably the most common misconception I come across is that coaching is the same as counseling or therapy, but they are, in fact, very different. Counseling looks to resolve past problems. Coaching focuses on the future. Counseling focuses on discovering the cause of past issues. Coaching focuses on creating action plans to achieve goals. Counseling is problem-focused. Coaching is goal-focused. Counseling is sought by people experiencing difficulties, and although coaching may be requested by someone having a problem, it is more often accessed by high achievers.

Workplace Coaching

In the workplace, coaching is focused on enabling employees to reach their fullest potential by identifying learning or developmental gaps (including limiting beliefs), coaching through performance issues and removing roadblocks to achieve their full potential. I believe that in the workplace you must become the coach that your employee needs, and that means having a flexible rather than static view of coaching. While I do believe that coaches should only ask questions rather than give advice, there are scenarios in work where that simply does not assist the employee, e.g., new hires. In some organizations, my coaching has incorporated elements of mentoring, feedback, training, and at times, counseling.

I personally don't like getting caught up in the definitions and instead focus on being the best coach that I can be. If an organization is serious about coaching, it is less about what coaching is or is not. Instead, it focuses on the desired outcomes they want to achieve. Focus more on what you want to achieve and less on how you want to achieve it.

I think it is also important to say that in much of my workplace coaching, elements of counseling or dealing with personal problems creep in. In fact, according to the 2015 International Coaching Federation, 97% of respondents said "no" to the question "Are you frequently hired to address personal issues?" Yet, 76% responded "yes" to "Have you ever assisted an executive with personal issues?"

Companies may not hire coaches to attend to issues relating to their employees' personal lives, but often personal matters do creep in, and I experience this all the time. It is not that the employee's intention is to bring up personal issues but that they get uncovered during the coaching session. I frequently experience scenarios where I am coaching a high potential employee, and we start to look at areas like work/life balance, time management, prioritization, and career planning, and all of these issues connect to the employee's personal world, particularly if they are in a relationship, and even more so if they have children.

I believe it is a great thing for companies to recognize their employees' external challenges and help them as much as is feasible to develop the skills to better manage these challenges—this can only serve to make them happier, more productive, and loyal team members.

Case Study: The Defense Acquisition University

A growing body of evidence shows that training and leadership development programs are more effective when they include a coaching component. Some purists believe that all leadership development should be done solely through coaching, particularly at the most senior levels, but I believe that training still plays an important part in the acquisition of new skills and can be enhanced by ongoing coaching.

The Defense Acquisition University (DAU) provides an exemplary model of how coaching can reinforce and improve an already best-in-class training and development program.

As the corporate university for the defense acquisition workforce of the US, the DAU provides in-person and virtual learning opportunities and leadership development to the 152,000 military and civilian professionals associated with the largest buying enterprise in the world. In late 2007, the DAU began to explore the possibility of adding a coaching service to its portfolio of offerings to improve acquisition outcomes and enhance the leadership capacity of key leaders.

With an annual procurement budget of $350bn, the defense acquisition operating environment demands a significant return on every investment of time, workforce, and money. The DAU's initiative has met this requirement with measurable results throughout the coaching program. The DAU has measured and tracked the workforce-wide impacts of its coaching program and estimates a nonfinancial return on investment of 330% and a financial return on investment of 743%.

Also, according to the International Coaching Federation (ICF) Global Coaching Client Study, companies that use or have used professional coaching for business reasons have a median return on investment of seven times their initial investment. Other expected benefits are:

- Increased productivity with 70% of coaching recipients experiencing improved work performance
- 61% improved business management
- 57% improved time management
- 51% improved team effectiveness

The ICF study also shows:

- Improved self-confidence (80%)
- Improved relationships (73%)
- Improved communication skills (72%)
- Improved work/life balance (67%)

The report states that the top three reasons coaches are engaged are:

1. To develop high potential talent or facilitate transition (48%)
2. To act as a sounding board (26%)
3. To address derailing behavior (12%)

I would agree with these results as I see most organizations using coaching services to focus on the development of their high potential talent because they recognize that a tailored and personalized one-to-one approach for these individuals gives better returns than traditional classroom training. Coaching is also a great retention tool for high potential talent as it demonstrates the value the company places on their development and their importance to the organization.

The ICF survey also examines what organizations look for when hiring a coach, and interestingly, there were very mixed results. Over 29% of respondents felt some sort of coaching certification or qualification would be required, and 28.5% said they do not look for any certification at all. I totally understand these responses because I believe certification of some kind is necessary to ensure your employees receive high-quality coaching from a trained professional. Yet if I really had to choose a coach for my own employees or to train my managers, I would look for someone who has extensive practical hands-on experience over a qualification any day. And if I could give you an additional bit of advice, I would ask to be coached by them before I would consider hiring them so that I can personally experience their coaching style, the extensiveness of their coaching tools, professionalism, etc.

The median cost of a workplace coach today is estimated at $500 per hour, so you want to make absolutely sure that you are hiring the right person in order to get the best possible return on investment and coaching experience for your employees.

The Logical Levels of Learning

I have always been curious about why great training courses sometimes do not help employees to successfully learn and deploy the skills which they have been trained on. The employee who attended the time management course and still is woefully disorganized. The manager that you sent on the emotional intelligence course who still can't seem to connect with his team. The high potential rising star, the one you know can make it all the way to the top, has come back from her confidence-building course and is still hiding at her desk in the far corner rarely making eye contact with anyone.

I'm sure you have plenty of examples of team members whose training seems to have let them and you down. I've attended some great training courses during my career, but oh, if I only knew then what I know now. I honestly believe that if I had had a coach starting in my late twenties, I could be ruling the world today! I haven't given up on that dream, but I can honestly say that most training courses that I have attended in the last ten years were a waste of the company's money. Harsh but true. If I had had a good coach, I would have worked on my self-confidence (or lack of), my challenges in being a female in male-dominated workplaces, and my tendencies to jump into things too quickly without thinking through my plan properly. That kind of coaching would have helped me enormously and made a massive difference to my levels of performance and productivity for the organizations I worked for.

I discovered the logical levels during Neuro-Linguistic Programming (NLP) training, and it really helped me understand the reasons and logic as to why training is not always the best solution for an individual's development. The concept of logical levels of learning and change was initially formulated as a mechanism in the behavioral sciences by anthropologist Gregory Bateson, based on Bertrand Russell's work in logic and mathematics. It was then adapted by Robert Dilts, and I have found it to be a great tool for exploring how and why we do what we do.

The logical levels look at our thinking across six levels:

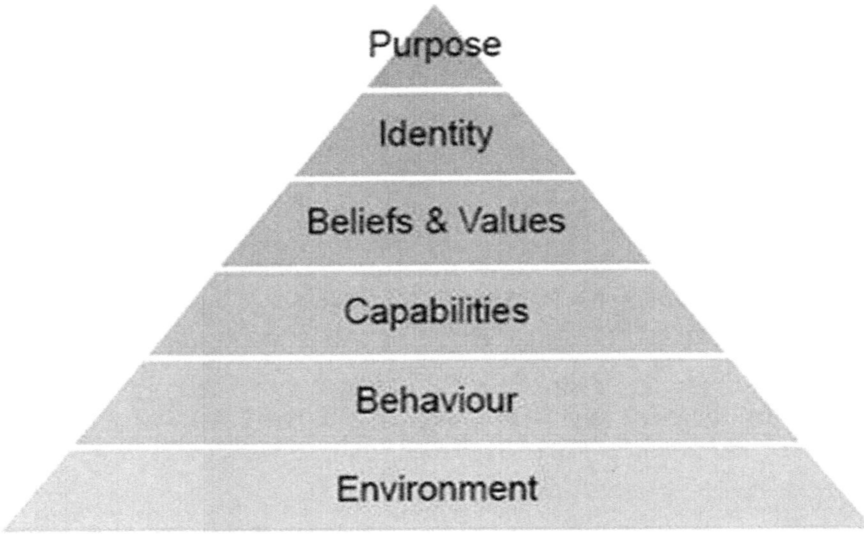

The Environment level relates to the external factors or conditions in which you live or work. Questions we would use at this level would be: Where did this happen? When did this happen? To whom did this happen? All relating to external factors to the individual.

The Behavior level refers to what you do in different settings or how exactly you behave in a particular context. Capabilities describe how you do what you do. What are your unique skills and strategies for taking action?

Beliefs and Values define why you do something, and they shape the way you perceive the world. Beliefs can be both empowering (e.g., I believe I will have a happy life), and limiting (e.g., I believe I will never have enough money to live comfortably.) Identity consolidates the system of beliefs and values into a sense of self. It defines who you think you are, as an individual or an organization. Purpose speaks to the connection you have to something bigger and greater than the individual. It relates to questions like: What is my purpose? For whom am I doing this? How will this help others?

Many learning and development programs target the Capabilities level, related to skills and strategies for taking action. For example, if someone in your team doesn't know how to use Microsoft Office—they don't yet have that skill—you can send them to a Microsoft Office course (or do it online). So far, so good.

But what about a different member of your team who withholds information from her colleagues. In this example, the individual is a high performer and a very engaged employee, but her colleagues have complained on multiple occasions that she is withholding critical information required for team decision-making. So, what logical level should we be targeting for a development solution? It could be Behavior; it could be Capability; and it could be Beliefs & Values. Well, we won't know until we find out more by talking to the individual directly.

I have a real-life example of this exact scenario, and when I spoke to the employee and raised the concerns her colleagues had made, she flat out refused that they were true. From her point of view, she always responded to every request for information, and she didn't understand why these comments would be made. I had requested evidence of this behavior from her colleagues because I don't believe in hearsay and like to fully understand the situation. I gave her one specific example of a request for information that had been made to her and had yet to be fulfilled. Her response was, "He doesn't need to know that. That's not his job. It's mine."

After continued coaching, it turned out that she felt that requests for certain information from her colleagues meant that they did not trust her ability to do her job well. She equated requests for information as a way for her colleagues to test her and try to catch her out. More importantly, she resisted giving them information because she herself lacked confidence in her own ability and felt she would be exposed if she gave information freely. This admission of a lack of self-confidence and lack of trust in her colleagues was followed by tears and a conversation about how stressed out she felt.

Now, at face value, we could have assumed that a little bit of team building might have solved this behavioral problem. Potentially, with a well-structured trust-building exercise, it may have given some relief to the individual, but it would not have solved the problem. The right development intervention for this person needed to happen at the Beliefs and Values level because she obviously had limiting beliefs about her abilities and her colleagues' intentions.

This is so important because companies risk wasting huge amounts of money on training that will not effectively address the issues, behaviors, or skills that they want to develop or solve. Only a coaching conversation could ever shine a light on these limiting beliefs that are the root cause of the behavior. This is not to say that training isn't at times the right solution. It often is, but the difference is that we fully understand the developmental challenge and goals before we decide the best learning intervention.

Limiting Beliefs

Limiting beliefs are beliefs that we hold that constrain us in some way. They hold us back from reaching our full potential. They are often about us and our identities, but they may also be about other people and the world in general. Limiting beliefs are simply assumptions about reality that just are not true. I would estimate that 90% of my workplace coaching sessions relate specifically to coaching an employee's limiting belief(s).

I recently coached an individual who started the coaching session saying he needed to be coached on his public speaking skills. When I asked him to elaborate further, he said that he gets extremely nervous when speaking in public and particularly hates when he is called to speak without being given time to prepare.

Dee: *How do you know you need to improve your public speaking skills?*

Coachee: *Well, because I feel very nervous when I have to speak publicly, and I feel that my nervousness detracts from my presentation.*

Dee: *Have you ever received any feedback on your presentation skills?*

Coachee: *Yes, and actually the feedback was nice.*

Dee: *Have you ever received any negative or constructive feedback on your presentation skills?*

Coachee: *No (long pause). That's strange. I never looked at it like that.*

Dee: *Looked at it like what?*

Coachee: *Nobody has ever told me I need to improve, and just last week my boss said I gave a very good presentation.*

Dee: *So, do you still feel like you need to improve your presentation skills?*

Coachee: *I'm not sure now—I feel a bit confused.*

Dee: *And confused is good. If you were sure about what you would like to focus on today, what might that be?*

Coachee: *(long pause) I would like to talk about my self-confidence.*

And the coaching session went on for about 45 minutes. We continued to peel away the layers, and as it turned out, it had nothing to do with presentation skills. We identified over eight limiting beliefs in that coaching session, none of which had any bearing on reality but were holding the individual back from reaching his full potential. Those eight limiting beliefs were:

1. I will be negatively judged no matter how well prepared I am.
2. I need to be extremely well prepared all the time just in case I can't answer someone's question.
3. I will always feel nervous when it comes to interacting with people more senior than me.
4. I don't think I'm good enough to be here.
5. I am afraid of being found out.
6. I lack charisma.
7. My colleagues think I am dull.
8. My English isn't fluent enough, so I come across as inarticulate at times.

Those are powerful beliefs to hold about oneself, and before the coaching session, this person was not aware at all that he felt this way. It is quite amazing how critical we are of ourselves. I do believe that most of us don't need constructive criticism because we have already done a good enough job of it ourselves and then some. We can be our own worst enemies, and this is why the identification of limiting beliefs is so important.

Other examples of limiting beliefs are:

- I lack motivation.
- I procrastinate too much.
- I don't have time.

- I don't have enough resources.
- It's too late to change.
- I have too many responsibilities.
- I have no clue what I'm supposed to be doing.
- I have no clue where to start.

We all have limiting beliefs, and I have found that most people can go through life being totally unaware of most of them. When coaching, I am always listening out for the "yes, but . . ." and the "I can't do that because . . ." The use of "but" and "because" are always signs of an underlying limiting belief.

If you want to quickly identify some of your own limiting beliefs, you can simply do this by answering these questions:

What am I not good at?

....

....

....

....

....

What are things that I believe I could never do or achieve?

....

....

....

....

....

....

A more powerful question that I frequently ask is, "What is stopping you from achieving your goals?"

....

....

....

....

....

....

The response to this question will always uncover one or more limiting beliefs.

It is important to understand the power that a limiting belief can hold over someone without them even being aware of it. Think of any goal that you have set for yourself, that you really want to achieve, but despite multiple attempts you just cannot achieve it—losing weight, getting fit, giving up smoking, better work/life balance, etc. There are limiting beliefs underpinning the lack of results that you want, and no amount of training is going to make a difference.

Most of today's leadership development programs target Behaviors (what you do), and the Skills and Capabilities level (how you do it). What we neglect to include in leadership development are the Beliefs and Values level and the Identity level which guide, influence, and impact what we do and how we do it.

For example, a leader who needs to improve her communication skills gets sent on a communication skills course. Straightforward, right? But this leader holds a limiting belief that her colleagues may think negatively of her for sharing some of her ideas. A communication skills course will not solve this issue. It would require a coaching intervention instead. That limiting belief could be identified, discussed, and addressed quickly, allowing the leader to become more self-aware and gain some useful insights on her limiting belief. She would also experience an increase in her confidence because through coaching she would have come up with a solution to this herself. (One of the signs of a very good coach is that they never give advice. They ask questions that allow the coachee to identify their issues and their solutions themselves.)

If you want to design truly effective development programs, then you must incorporate coaching solutions to the identification of limiting beliefs that are holding your leaders and their teams back from reaching their full potential. This will serve to dramatically improve the results of your training programs, the performance of the individual, and your organization's business results.

Identifying Limiting Beliefs

There are multiple ways to identify limiting beliefs, and I will share one of the easier ways. I like to call this the "because, because, because" exercise.

"Because" is an interesting word because when it appears in a sentence, it is usually followed by a reason (or an excuse if I am to be totally honest):

- I can't go to the gym because I don't have enough time.
- I can't start my own business because I can't afford to take the risk.
- I can't get the promotion because my boss doesn't like me.
- I can't save money because I'm not disciplined enough.

Each time you hear "because" you are going to hear a reason (or excuse) for the statement that comes just before it. The only exception is when it includes a description of reality that is factual (e.g., I am too hot because it is 33-degree Celsius today; or I was late for work because there was a car accident on the highway).

Limiting beliefs are descriptions of what we believe to be true, but in reality, we are confusing these beliefs with fact. For example, you may believe that you will be held back in your career because you are not charismatic or inspirational, but in all likelihood, that belief is not based on any fact or evidence. "I am not charismatic" is not a description of reality (even though it may be confused with one).

The phrase "I am not charismatic" is a real giveaway here. My first question to that statement of belief would be "says who?" This is a powerful question to uncover that the belief has been self-created.

I could also choose to ask questions like:

- How do you know you are not charismatic?
- So, there isn't one time in your entire life that you haven't been charismatic, ever?
- When did you decide to believe that you are uncharismatic?

All these questions serve to shake the foundations of the belief. For a belief to be a fact there must be visible and unquestionable evidence or proof. Without that evidence, the belief starts to crumble as the individual begins to question its truth.

So how can we use "because" to expose someone's limiting beliefs?

1. **Choose a problem or challenge that you would like to focus on. It could be something like:**

   I will never get the promotion I want because there is always someone who outperforms me.

   ....

   ....

   ....

   ....

   ....

2. **Write down all the possible reasons for this belief followed by the word "because":**

   State the problem out loud, ending with "because," and write down whatever comes into your head, without any judgment.

   I will never get the promotion because my colleagues are better than me.
   I will never get the promotion because I don't stand out when compared to my peers.
   I will never get the promotion because nobody seems to recognize my value or even notice what I do.

I will never get the promotion because I have reached my potential and just have to be content where I am.

Keep going until you can no longer come up with any responses or reasons. Don't analyze your answers at this point. Just go as quickly as you can and get as many reasons as you can.

....

....

....

....

....

....

....

....

....

....

3. Prioritize the beliefs

Work through your list of reasons saying each one out loud. Give the reason a truth score from 0–10, where 0 is false and 10 is true. (This is how true it is in terms of how it feels rather than how logically true it is.) Repeat this process and then sort this list from the highest truth score to the lowest.

....

....

....

....

....

....

....

....

....

....

Now you have a list of limiting beliefs that can be worked on.

It's also important to note that the beliefs identified are probably related, and by working on the highest scoring belief first, there is a strong possibility that it will resolve many of the other lower-scoring limiting beliefs. Just like killing two birds with one stone.

So, what can you do to resolve those pesky limiting beliefs?

Well, in many cases, once the belief has been identified and the fact that there is not enough evidence to support the belief has been clarified, the belief will give way itself. I cannot overstate how quickly these beliefs can disappear once the coachee recognizes that the belief has not been built on fact, and the coachee will just disregard the belief as nonsense.

I find the easiest way to move forward is to shake the evidence foundations of the belief with questions like "Who says?" and "How do you know?" and "When did you decide this?" There is also a possibility that someone is holding onto a limiting belief because they derive some pleasure from it. For example, I may choose to believe that I will never get the promotion because I'm actually quite happy where I am, but I don't **want** to admit it.

Moving forward, it's critical to determine what the individual is gaining by holding onto each of the limiting beliefs. If they are showing resistance to releasing the limiting belief, you can ask them:

- How might you be deriving pleasure by holding onto this limiting belief?

- With what good intention does this belief provide you?
- What value are you gaining by holding onto this belief?

To replace a limiting belief with a more empowering belief, you will either need to convince your coachee that the value they are deriving from this limiting belief isn't required any longer, or a new empowering belief must in some way fill the void. So, you either fill this void or eliminate the void altogether.

Team Exercise: Three Little Words

It can be very useful to get the wider team involved in understanding and identifying limiting beliefs in themselves and others. In fact, this makes your job as a coaching leader much easier! It also brings coaching into the day-to-day of how you operate as a leader, and it teaches your team some of the basics of coaching. I like learning activities that don't need to be planned far in advance but happen fluidly throughout the day. Effortless.

This is a very simple example of one of the ways I incorporate coaching into my day-to-day operations. I can't really call it an exercise as it doesn't have a start and end time. Rather it's a leadership/coaching tool that I incorporate into my own leadership style.

Purpose

1. Improve use of language.
2. Identify limiting beliefs and excuses.
3. Encourage team spirit and support of each other.
4. Teach basic coaching skills.

Description

Brief the team on what limiting beliefs are, how they can hold them back, how they can be identified, and the benefits derived by resolving them. You can use any of the content from this chapter to do this. Advise the team that from here onwards everyone is to pay particular attention when they hear the words "but" and "because," either from themselves or someone else in the team (including you). You can explain that the reason for specifically choosing these words is because they generally come before an excuse and/or a limiting belief, and you want them to start identifying their own limiting beliefs and the beliefs held by the entire team that could be holding them back.

But

When someone says the word "but," they need to change it to "and." (e.g., instead of "I wanted to do that, but I couldn't because I got distracted," it would change to "I wanted to do that, and I couldn't because I got distracted.") As soon as you say the word "but," the other person immediately forgets the part about you "wanted to do" because they are only listening for what comes after the "but." This is particularly important when giving feedback. Many times we hear feedback like "You did this really well, but . . ." or "I'd really love to give you that salary increase, but . . ." As soon as we hear a "but" in a sentence, we practically delete everything that came before the "but" and focus only on what comes after it. This makes it a very important word. This lesson instills this new language pattern in your team. You should encourage them to point out when they hear someone else say "but" (in their team that is).

Because

The approach with "because" is slightly different in that we don't replace the word "because" with anything, but just start to notice what comes after the "because" and more specifically what comes after "because" in a negative statement like "I can't do that because I'm not able to." When you hear a negative "because," you ask the person (or yourself) one of these questions:

- How do you know (everything after the because)?
- How do you know you're not able to?
- Who says (everything after the because)?
- Who says you're not able to?
- What if (everything after the because), what would you do first?
- What if you were able to, what would you do first?

Now in some cases, it will be a fact, and that's perfectly fine! The purpose here is to identify potential limiting beliefs and start to become more evidence-based in our thinking and speech. So, if one of the team says something like "We can't achieve that goal because we don't have enough budget" (and this could be a fact but no harm in seeing if we can get creative), I would respond with "What if we did have enough budget, what would you do first?" This instantly moves the person into forward action and looking at the challenge from a different perspective—a more resourceful perspective.

Try

And last but not least, "try." You can just go ahead and ban this word completely! As the all-powerful and knowing Yoda so wisely said, "Do or do not. There is no try." Personally, I can't stand the word "try," and most of my team members can testify to that. People who say "I will try" have given themselves permission to fail. No matter what happens, they can always claim that they "tried," and that is not good enough in a high-performing team. To make it exciting, you can set up a "try" jar, and whoever is heard saying "try" most often puts an agreed-upon sum of money in the jar.

The Communication Framework

How We Communicate

Albert Mehrabian (born 1939 to an Armenian family in Iran), currently Professor Emeritus of Psychology, UCLA, has become well known for his publications on the importance of verbal and nonverbal messages. His findings on conflicting messages of feelings and attitudes have been misinterpreted worldwide and have also become known as the 7%-38%-55% Rule.

In his studies, Mehrabian comes to two conclusions. First, that there are three elements in any face-to-face communication:

- Words
- Tone of voice
- Nonverbal behavior, e.g., facial expressions.

Second, the nonverbal components are particularly important for communicating feelings and attitude, especially when they are incongruent. When words disagree with the tone of voice and nonverbal behavior, people tend to give more credence to the tonality and nonverbal behavior.

It is not the case that the nonverbal component conveys the bulk of the message even though this is how his findings are frequently misinterpreted. For example, when delivering a presentation, the textual content is provided entirely verbally, but the nonverbal cues are also important in conveying the speaker's attitude towards what they are saying, notably their beliefs or convictions.

Words account for 7%; the tone of voice accounts for 38%; and body language accounts for 55%. For effective and meaningful communication, these three parts of the message need to support each other. They have to be congruent.

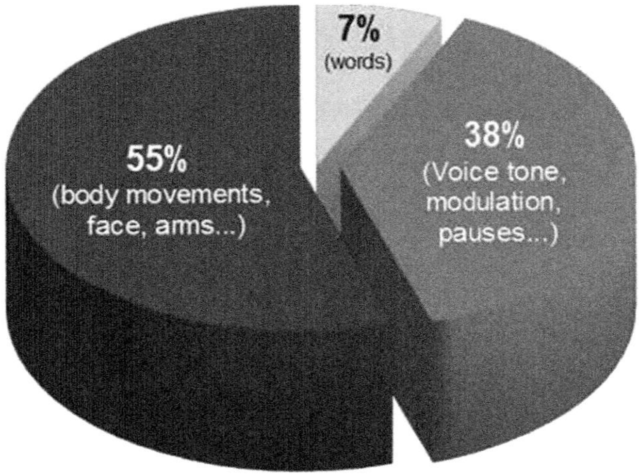

You know when someone is incongruent because their body language doesn't match what they have said or their tone of voice. It's like somebody asking, "How are you?" while making no eye contact with you and saying it in a sarcastic tone of voice. The words are not in alignment with the body or voice.

As a coach, signs of incongruence are telling, and you should get curious when you see evidence of them. It is important to notice them because the coachees may not be aware of it themselves, and it can impact the actions (or lack thereof) that they take during and after the coaching session.

A perfect example of this is a client I was coaching recently. We were discussing commitments that she was making towards some change she wanted to take effect in her life. She set a goal for herself, and when I asked her if she was totally committed to this aim, she said "yes" but her facial expressions showed signs of fear. When I brought this to her attention, she told me she was scared of not having the necessary time to commit to some of the actions we discussed. So we were able to take another look at the goal and set a more realistic target for her.

I knew we had set a congruent goal when she started to sit up straighter in the chair. She began to smile and expressed excitement about taking action. I checked her commitment again, and this time she sounded far more confident—words, tone, and body language.

The following example should help illustrate incongruence in verbal and nonverbal communication.

- Verbal: "I do not have a problem with you!"
- Nonverbal: person avoids eye contact, looks anxious, has closed body language, etc.

In this example, it becomes more likely that the listener will trust the predominant form of communication, which to Mehrabian's findings is the nonverbal impact of tone plus gestures (38% + 55%), rather than the literal meaning of the words (7%). This is known as the "7%-38%-55% Rule."

Paying attention to all three forms of communication is key to becoming a successful coach, as focusing on the words alone means you may miss out on some important and often critical information. Always be on the lookout for congruence, and when you spot incongruence, don't be afraid to bring it to the attention of your coachee in the form of feedback.

Sensory Acuity

Sensory acuity is your ability to notice even the smallest changes in a person's verbal and nonverbal language. Developing your sensory acuity greatly assists in correctly identifying congruence and is also a key component in developing rapport, which we will discuss later. New coaches often make the mistake of trying to read too much into someone's body language (i.e., just because someone has their arms crossed does not necessarily mean they are defensive. They may just be cold!) It is important to notice when someone displays a change in their body language, and that can be something as small as going from speaking in a normal tone of voice to reducing the volume slightly, or from sitting upright in the chair to leaning back or forwards. What is happening when they display the change? Your job is to get curious and keep an open mind. The best coaches never judge or assume. They observe, listen, and respond.

Here are just some of the things you can notice about people's responses:

Voice

- tempo
- volume
- pitch
- tone
- modulation
- timbre
- type of words used

Inclination (of the spine; general posture and gesture)

- slumped or straight
- leaning forwards, upright, or back
- symmetrical/asymmetrical to left or right
- range and speed of gestures
- micro-muscle movements

Breathing
- rate
- depth
- location in body

Eyes
- movements
- pupil dilation
- redness
- watering
- direction

Skin
- color
- muscle tone
- size of areas (e.g., lips)
- shiny/dull
- goose-pimples

The easiest way to develop your sensory acuity is to practice, practice, practice. When I started out, I would (and actually still do) watch people in meetings, in airports, in the queue at the supermarket. I would focus on all the sensory acuity points and then notice any of the changes, no matter how small. A little trick that worked for me was to start from the top of the head and move downwards so that I wouldn't miss anything:

Head: How is the head placed—is it tilted, straight, turned to the speaker, down?

> Are there frown lines on the forehead? Between the eyebrows.
> What direction are the eyes going when the person is talking?
> How much eye contact are they making?
> What is their rate/speed of blinking?
> What is the color and texture of their skin?
> If speaking, what is the tonality/pace/speed?

If speaking, what words are they using to describe things—visual, auditory, kinesthetic?

Neck: If speaking, are they speaking in a strained, high-pitched manner?
Chest: From where are they breathing?
Body: How are they moving—the entire body?
If seated, how are they sitting?
Are they gesticulating?
Are they holding or playing with anything (e.g., holding a pen in their hands)?
If with someone else, how much physical distance is between the two?
What kind of clothes are they wearing?

It's amazing how much information you can pick up just by focusing intently on someone. Now be careful not to be stalker-like with this, as staring at strangers, in fact, staring at anyone isn't advisable. So, please be sure to be discreet. I find that when you are coaching in the workplace you can focus less on your sensory acuity since you are working in close quarters with your team and will probably already be very familiar with their patterns of language, body language, communication quirks, etc. That said, you can never develop this skill enough. So practice, practice, practice!

The Power of Questions

"To be or not to be, that is the question." And what a great question it is. It's a powerful question. "To be or not to be?" You might ask, "To be what?" But that doesn't really matter, does it? Because we can all apply our own meanings or our own contexts to the question.

"To be or not to be?" How would you answer that question right now? I asked that question on my Facebook page, and the overwhelming response was "to be."

Or maybe you prefer "If not now, then when?" I use this question with people who are using time or lack of time as an excuse to not take action.

Tony Robbins says that "successful people ask better questions, and as a result, they get better answers." Makes total sense. But how do you know if your questions are good, and if you think you could be asking better questions, then what specifically do you need to do? What makes a good or powerful question?

A powerful question has several different components:

1. It is almost always an open rather than closed question in that the question cannot be responded to with just a yes or no answer.
2. More often than not, it is a very simple question and uncomplicated in its structure (e.g., What do you want? or Why is that important?)
3. A powerful question elicits a response made up of more than information, facts, or descriptions. It causes the coachee to uncover a blind spot and learn something new about themselves.
4. It also causes the coachee to do additional self-discovery, raising their curiosity and digging deeper than might generally be the case.

You will know when you have asked a powerful question because you'll be told directly "that's a great question," and/or you will notice the coachee pause, reflect and internally search for an answer. I am discovering new powerful questions every single day. I find them everywhere—on the television, listening to colleagues' conversations, reading coaching articles and blogs. They are everywhere. I often find that new coaches get intimidated about their ability to ask powerful questions, and like any standout skill, it is developed over time. I remind them that people love to talk about themselves, so getting asked any interesting question and having someone genuinely listen to the answer is already a great experience for a coachee. You will develop a treasure trove of powerful questions over time, and before you know it, you will intuitively know the best question to ask at the right time.

In the meantime, I have put together a selection of great questions to get you started.

Questions for when you want to get to know someone better (in the workplace)

1. Tell me about yourself.
2. What is your favorite thing about your career?
3. What is the biggest challenge you face in your career?
4. What does your child want to be when he/she grows up?
5. If you could choose to do anything for a day, what would it be?
6. If you could only eat one meal for the rest of your life, what would it be? Why?
7. What is your proudest accomplishment?
8. Is there anything or anyone standing in the way of achieving your goals?
9. What would you want to be doing in five years? At the mid-point of your career? At the end of it?
10. How can I help you achieve your goals?

Questions for new members of your team

1. Tell me about yourself.
2. Who is the best manager you've had up to now? What did you like most about them?
3. Who is the worst manager you've had up to now? What specifically did you not like about them?
4. Do you have any role models? What do you like most about him/her?

5. What are your career aspirations?
6. If I could wave a magic wand and grant you one wish right now, what would that wish be?
7. What is important to you about HOW I give you feedback?
8. If I must give you constructive feedback related to your performance, how would you like me to do that?
9. When you have feedback for me, HOW will you give it to me?
10. If you are having a problem at work, how will you let me know?
11. How do you like to be recognized when you've done a great job?
12. Are you an introvert or an extrovert? Why do you identify with that?
13. Are you a big picture thinker or do you prefer lots of detail?
14. Would you describe yourself as being a private person, a social butterfly, or something else entirely?
15. What else do I need to know about you to make sure we have the best possible working relationship?
16. Is there anything you would like to know about me?

Questions when being asked for advice

1. What have you come up with so far?
2. What are the options?
3. If your colleague were to ask you the same question, what would you advise them?
4. If I could guarantee you 100% success, what would you decide to do?
5. What does your gut tell you?
6. If you already knew the answer, what would it be?
7. If I weren't here, what would you decide to do?
8. Do you know anyone else who has solved a similar problem? Have you spoken to them?
9. What is the worst that can happen if you decide on the solution yourself?
10. What is stopping you from making this decision yourself?

Ice breaker questions to kick off a meeting

1. If life is so short, why do we do so many things we don't like and like so many things we don't do?
2. When it's all said and done, will you have said more than you've done?
3. What is the one thing you'd most like to change about the world?
4. If happiness was the national currency, what kind of work would make you rich?
5. If the average human life span was 40 years, how would you live your life differently?
6. What is something you know you do differently than most people?
7. What one thing have you not done that you really want to do? What is holding you back?
8. Are you holding onto something you need to let go of?
9. Why are you, you?
10. What are you most grateful for?
11. Would you rather lose all your old memories or never be able to make new ones?
12. What is your happiest childhood memory? What makes it so special?
13. If not now, then when?
14. If you haven't achieved it yet, what do you have to lose?
15. What would you do differently if you knew nobody would judge you?

Questions for brainstorming or when looking for alternative solutions

1. What do we want to achieve?
2. What is important about what we want to do?
3. What does success look like?
4. Do we have other examples of success?
5. How else can we do this?
6. What options have we not yet considered?
7. What could we do differently?
8. How can we improve?
9. What is the first step we need to take?
10. How will we measure success?

Questions when making excuses or procrastinating about taking action

1. What is stopping you?
2. What is the worst that can happen?
3. If not now, then when?
4. What are you waiting for?
5. What will happen if you do take action?
6. What won't happen if you do take action?
7. What will happen if you don't take action?
8. What won't happen if you don't take action?
9. If you were guaranteed 100% success, what is the first step you would take?
10. If you knew what was holding you back from taking action, what might that be?

Questions to ask your manager

1. How would you like me to keep you up to date on work progress?
2. What is the best way for me to give you bad news?
3. What annoys you/gets on your nerves (at work)?
4. When I don't agree with you, what is the best way for me to give you that feedback?
5. How will you let me know when I am doing well?
6. How do you prefer to give me feedback on areas I need to improve on?
7. What does success look or sound like to you in terms of our working relationship?
8. What else do I need to know about your work/communication style to ensure we have a great working relationship?
9. Is there anything you would like me to share with you about my work/communication style?
10. If there was one question that you would like me to ask you that I haven't asked you already, what would that question be? (When they tell you the question, ask them the question back.)

Career development questions

Current Role

1. What do you like most about your current job?
2. What would you like to do more of?
3. What do you like the least about your current job?
4. What would you like to do less of?
5. What skills does your current job require?
6. What is your current skill level in those areas?
7. What parts of your job challenge you the most?
8. What parts of your job excite you the most?
9. What skills do you have that differentiate you from your colleagues?
10. What feedback have you received about your performance? (positive and constructive)

Professional Growth Goals

1. Where would you like to be professionally two or three years from now?
2. What are your long-term career goals?
3. What is important to you about your career?
4. What are your career values?
5. How do these career goals fit into your wider personal aspirations and goals (e.g., family, finances, and hobbies)?
6. What would you need to achieve now to accomplish this?
7. What new responsibilities or challenges would move you ahead?
8. What are the strengths, weaknesses, opportunities and threats to you achieving your career goals?
9. What might stop you from achieving your career goals?
10. What are your top three professional goals for the next 12 months?

Learning & Development

1. Is there something more that you could do that would make a greater contribution to our organization?
2. Is there a new task or role you could take on that would make better use of your talents?
3. What additional value could you provide? What would it take to "release" this?
4. What are you not "allowed" to do that you could do and would like to do?
5. What challenges would you like to face that might help you grow?
6. What is the one skill that you don't currently consider a strength that you would really like to develop?
7. If you could improve one process, which would it be? How would it be different?
8. What do you want to be remembered for in this job?
9. Who do you wish you knew in our organization to develop you further in your job?
10. What do you need from me to help you in your development?

Communication (Mental Map) Preferences

We experience the world we live in through our primary sensory systems or the five senses—seeing, hearing, feeling, smelling, and tasting. The sensory modalities by which people encode, organize, store, and attach meaning to perceptual input are referred to as representational systems or mental maps. Many people have a preferred mental map, and when using that map, they will easily derive meaning themselves. When they meet with someone with the same preferred map, they will often feel a quick and mutual connection, or rapport, precisely because they have the same communication preferences and are literally speaking the same language.

The notion of learning style is an acknowledgment that people learn in different ways. Different people develop their sensory capabilities to varying degrees. Some people are naturally visual. Some people are more verbal and can speak and articulate experiences with ease, while others may struggle with words. And some people are very feeling-oriented and learn by doing. We habitually make assumptions that others have the same cognitive abilities that we do, but this often is not the case. In communicating with others, matching their preferred mental map is an important method of establishing rapport and ensuring that they will understand what you are communicating.

In summary, different mental maps may be used to enhance learning and communication in many ways:

1. Appealing to their strengths—matching the mental map that is most used and valued by the type of learners.
2. Strengthening their weakness—using an under-utilized or not often used mental map to stimulate new ways of thinking.
3. Emphasizing their mental map most appropriate or most suited to a particular cognitive process or type of activity.

We access information through our senses: see (visual), hear (auditory), feel (kinesthetic), taste (gustatory), and smell (olfactory). For our purposes, to communicate efficiently and create rapport, we will focus on the visual, auditory, kinesthetic, and auditory digital communication styles or mental maps. To process and store this information, we make pictures in our minds of what we believe we have seen, sounds of what we think we have heard, emotions of what we think we have felt, etc.

We use all four mental maps, and we have a strong preference for one in particular. For example, when we learn something new, some of us may prefer to see it performed; others like to hear or be told how to do it; others choose to get a feeling for it or put it into practice; and yet others aim to make sense of it. It is important to note that one mental map is not better than another, and your preferred mental map may change over time. I have found that people at the top of their profession typically can use all the mental maps, and they have the flexibility to choose those that are the most appropriate for that context.

The following questionnaire will allow you to determine your own preferred mental maps. Remember, this has no right or wrong answer and no perfect score. We each possess all four mental maps, and we will use them differently in different contexts. Your preferences, however, are important to understand, particularly as a coach. The best coaches can maneuver between the different mental maps whenever necessary.

Communication Preferences Questionnaire

For each item of the following statements, please place a number next to EVERY phrase. Use the following to indicate your preferences:

4 = Closest to describing you

3 = Next best description of you

2 = Quite descriptive of you

1 = Least descriptive of you

1. I make important decisions based on:
   a. ______ my intuition and gut-level feelings.
   b. ______ what sounds the best to me.
   c. ______ what looks best to me.
   d. ______ detailed review and analysis of the issues.

2. During an argument, I am most likely to be influenced by:
   a. _______the other person's tone of voice.
   b. ______ whether or not I can see the other person's point of view.
   c. ______ the logic of the other person's argument.
   d. ______ whether or not I am in touch with the other person's true feelings.

3. I most easily communicate what is going on with me by:
   a. ______ the way I dress and look.
   b. ______ the feelings I share.
   c. _______the words I choose.
   d. ______ my tone of voice.

4. It is easier for me to:
   a. ______ find the ideal volume and tuning on a stereo system.
   b.______ select the most intellectually relevant point in an interesting subject.
   c. ______ choose the most comfortable furniture.
   d. ______ select rich, attractive color combinations.

5\.
   a. ______ I am very attuned to the sounds of my surroundings.
   b. ______ I am very adept at making sense of new facts and data.
   c. ______ I am very sensitive to the way articles of clothes feel on my body.
   d. ______ I have a strong response to colors and to the way a room looks.

6.

a. _____ I love to listen to music.

b. _____ I enjoy viewing art galleries and doing window shopping.

c. _____ I feel compelled to dance to loud music.

d. _____ I treasure moments of inner reflection.

7.

a. _____ I tend to answer questions using my gut feelings.

b. _____ I would rather take an oral (spoken) test than a written one.

c. _____ I get very irritated when there are no clear visual aids.

d. _____ I need to go "inside" and rationalize with myself about most new learning.

8.

a. _____ I have an analytical mind that talks to itself frequently.

b. _____ I have been told that I have a great speaking voice.

c. _____ I have a keen sense of touching and feeling things.

d. _____ My confidence increases when I look good.

9.

a. _____ I can resolve problems more quickly when I talk aloud to myself.

b. _____ I would rather be shown an illustration than have something explained to me.

c. _____ I find myself holding or touching things as they are being explained.

d. _____ Quiet moments of inner self-talk are essential for me to make a good decision.

10.

a. _____ I find that I can accurately sum up others just by their appearance.

b. _____ I can usually determine sincerity by the tone of a person's voice.

c. _____ I tend to detach myself from others to evaluate them accurately.

d. _____ The way others shake hands with me means a lot to me.

11.

a. _____ I can hear even the slightest noise that my car makes.

b. _____ It is important that my car is kept neat and clean, inside and out.

c. _____ I like a car that feels good when I drive it.

d. _____ The quietness of a car is important as it allows me to hear myself think.

12.

a. _____ I enjoy people watching.

b. _____ Others tell me that I'm easy to talk to.

c. _____ I tend to touch people when I'm talking.

d. _____ I love the challenge of answering my questions inwardly.

13.

a. _____ I can't remember what people look like; however, I usually have familiar feelings that I've met them before.

b. _____ I am somewhat aware of what voices sound like on the phone as well as face-to-face.

c. _____ I often remember what someone looked like but not remember the person's name.

d. _____ I usually have to talk to myself internally until I sense the right name.

14.

a. _____ I would rather have an idea explained to me than to read it.

b. _____ I learn best when I can analyze things by reasoning with myself.

c. _____ I like to participate in activities rather than watch.

d. _____ I enjoy seminars more if they use powerful visual aids.

15.

a. _____ I am patient in waiting for others to finish their sentences.

b. _____ I find myself judging others by their facial expressions.

c. _____ I feel positive or negative towards others, sometimes without knowing why.
d. _____ I tend to distance myself from others to make better judgments logically.

16.

a. _____ I exercise because of the way I feel afterward.
b. _____ I work out consistently to stay in good shape.
c. _____ I exercise because I love the compliments others give me.
d. _____ I exercise so that I can hear myself say "Awesome!"

17.

a. _____ It's important that my house is clean and tidy. It gives me a picture of orderliness.
b. _____ I like a house with rooms that are quiet enough for self-evaluation.
c. _____ It's all-important to me that a house feels cozy and comfortable.
d. _____ It's crucial that my house is conducive to listening to music.

18.

a. _____ I like to match the way people talk.
b. _____ I make a list of things I need to do each day.
c. _____ I've been told that I'm well-coordinated.
d. _____ My abilities in logical reasoning are well known among my friends.

19.

a. _____ I like hands-on, do-it-yourself activities.
b. _____ I enjoy having interesting conversations with my friends.
c. _____ I like to go to the movies or watch television.
d. _____ I like reading thought-provoking books that encourage me to reason with myself.

COMMUNICATION STYLE SCORE SHEET				
Question #	VISUAL	AUDITORY	KINESTHETIC	AUD. DIGITAL
1	C	B	A	D
2	B	A	D	C
3	A	D	B	C
4	D	A	C	B
5	D	A	C	B
6	B	A	C	D
7	C	B	A	D
8	D	B	C	A
9	B	A	C	D
10	A	B	D	C
11	B	A	C	D
12	A	B	C	D
13	C	B	A	D
14	D	A	C	B
15	B	A	C	D
16	B	C	A	D
17	A	D	C	B
18	B	A	C	D
19	C	B	A	D

Maximum score for representational system = 76, Lowest = 19

People have different ways of communicating their experiences. Some express themselves in pictures; others talk about how things sound to them; and others speak about how things feel. A Mental Map is a powerful way of expressing the thought patterns, pictures, and associations that already exist in the brain.

VISUAL

Individuals with a visual preference process the world through what they see. It is estimated that at least 40% of the population have a visual preference. Certain characteristics can help you identify whether an individual has a strong visual preference.

Regarding their body language, their head is always tilted slightly upwards so that they can take in as much information through their eyes as possible. They always want the best possible view of the world around them and can get frustrated if their view is blocked because that stops them from processing as much visual information as they need. The Visuals maintain good eye contact, and when asked questions, they tend to look upwards. When asking a Visual a question, it helps to view their way of accessing internal information or memories as a form of cinema (e.g., when you ask them how their weekend was, they will start to 'picture' their weekend; they will replay the movie of their weekend in their head—visually). As a result, Visuals have a great visual memory. If your partner has a Visual preference, they will remember how you looked or what you wore the first time they met you, but they may not necessarily remember what you spoke about.

When Visuals speak, they do so with a higher-pitched voice. So much so that it can sound strained at times. They talk in quick bursts—staccato. As the Visuals are so focused on the information they are taking in through their eyes, they are not so concerned about what is coming out of their mouths (often to the frustration of their Auditory counterparts). When speaking, the Visuals will use visual sensory words to describe people, things, and places (e.g., see, look, picture, view). You will hear them say things like:

- That looks good to me!
- Let's get a bird's eye view.
- Look at the big picture first.
- Then we can focus on the detail.
- He was a sight for sore eyes.
- The clarity of his presentation style revealed brilliant insight and cleared the fog.

- I see what you mean.
- I am looking closely at the idea.
- We see eye to eye.
- I have a hazy notion.
- He has a blind spot.
- Show me what you mean.
- You'll look back on this and laugh.

Examples of the kinds of words Visuals will use include:

Angle, appear, clarity, demonstrate, examine, focus, foresee, glance, hindsight, illustrate, image, look, notice, observe, outlook, picture, pinpoint, scene, see, show, sight, sketchy, vague, view, vision, watch.

Visuals' gestures tend to be sweeping and unpredictable. They draw the world with their hands to better explain their thoughts and feelings. Think of someone at work who is the first up to the whiteboard to draw out ideas even when they are not asked to do so. They do this because this is the most efficient manner for them to process the information being discussed in the meeting. The same can be said for those who are quick to grab pen and paper and draw out their thoughts when they are talking to you.

It is also important to note that they like to keep a physical distance from others. Why? Well, if they stand or sit too close to you, it restricts their view. They will stay about arms width away from you so that they can see you head to toe. This is important when coaching a Visual regarding seating arrangements because sitting too close to the Visual may negatively impact rapport.

Other characteristics worth noting are:

- They are big picture thinkers.
- Their general appearance is neat with good color and shape coordination.
- They learn best through watching and reading.
- Their challenge is remembering verbal instructions.

Visuals will get distracted when looking at something that is visually displeasing. I can give you a personal example of one of my Visual idiosyncrasies. When reviewing a document, whether my own or someone else's, I'm put off by spelling mistakes and poor formatting. So much so that I have to correct the document as I am reading it. Otherwise, I just find it too distracting to process. Does anybody resonate with that?

Another great example I have is from a course I delivered a few years back. I was facilitating a leadership course, and I noticed a lady at the front of the class who seemed very distracted. She wasn't paying attention when I spoke, and she kept looking at the gentleman sitting beside her. When I got a bit closer to her, I realized that the gentleman had some dandruff on his shoulder (his jacket was black, so it was quite obvious), and this is what the lady kept looking at. I obviously couldn't intervene in this little exchange because it would have been embarrassing for both parties. It turns out I didn't need to because during the first coffee break, I witnessed the same lady, while speaking to the gentleman, gently graze his shoulder, wiping away said dandruff. The gentleman seemed confused by this but didn't react. And I do believe that she did not want to cause him any embarrassment, but the visual was just too distracting for her not to do anything about it.

We all experience this, although in less extreme terms, all the time. The last time someone fixed your collar, told you to tuck your shirt in or wiped a hair away from your face—these are the Visuals putting the world in order. Their neat, organized, coordinated order. Their love of visual order is often represented by an immaculate and tidy working space, or if they find disorder, they are quick to tidy up. At lunch, they will unconsciously line up the silverware on their table so that everything is aligned, straight, even, and ordered. If you are coaching someone with a high visual preference, you can use the following guidelines so that you have a better chance of creating high levels of rapport:

1. Use illustrations to explain concepts and ideas.
2. Keep pen and paper (colored markers are even better) so that they can draw their illustrations.
3. Use visually descriptive words, and don't be afraid to use your arms and hands to draw these words out. It will add more power to your communication.
4. They will learn best through watching and reading so it can be a good idea to give them something to read before and after the coaching session.

5. If you don't have a high Visual preference yourself, you will need to speed up your tempo. Pay attention to match their speed and tone of voice.
6. Always give them the big picture first.
7. Minimize any possible visual distractions. You will need to be conscious of your clothing and make sure the room you are coaching in is neat and tidy.
8. Maintain and match their eye contact.
9. Make sure to give them space. You will not want to sit too close to them.

AUDITORY

The Auditories process the world through what they hear, and it is estimated that they make up 30% of the population. Just as the Visuals access information and memories visually like replaying a movie, Auditories access information and memories like sound bites or MP3s. They have excellent auditory recall with an uncanny ability to remember everything that was said in a conversation years ago.

You can identify the Auditory preference in many different ways. They tend to listen to a conversation with their head turned towards the speaker so that their ear is facing the speaker's face. This makes sense when they want to capture as much sound as possible. Because they have their head/ear turned to the speaker, there tends to be less eye contact than with a Visual. The Auditories will look away to avoid distraction. They want to focus on what they are hearing rather than what they are seeing.

When you ask an Auditory a question, they will look to their ears as they access their internal audio files before responding. When they speak, they do so with a very even tone and rhythmic tempo. They make every effort to ensure they sound tonally right and enunciate clearly. They will use sensory words related to sound—hear, talk, listen. You will often hear them use phrases like:

- That sounds great! It's music to my ears!
- I'm sure what I have to say will resonate with you.

- This doesn't sound right to me.
- We're on the same wavelength.
- The place was humming with activity.
- Turn a deaf ear.
- That rings a bell!
- Take a moment to tune into the words I'm using, and you'll get the idea loud and clear.

Examples of other auditory sensory words are:

Announce, articulate, communicate, converse, discuss, gossip, hear, hush, interview, listen, loud, mention, proclaim, pronounce, ring, say, silence, sound, speak, speechless, talk, tell, tone, utter, vocal, voice.

Their body language is gentle and flowing, and their gestures tend to move in support and in time with what they are saying. They also verbally repeat what they have just heard which may be off-putting for someone who is not auditory. It can seem as though they are not paying attention to the conversation whereas their preference is to repeat things out loud so that they can hear them again, thus helping them to process and understand better.

The Auditory person will stand closer to others to listen better and can easily be distracted by sounds. They can hear a pin drop and will be put off by background noise that may not bother anyone else.

They learn best through listening, talking, and discussion.

To successfully create rapport with someone who has a high Auditory preference you can:

1. Use auditory descriptive words when speaking.
2. Maintain rhythm while talking and make an additional effort to enunciate clearly.
3. Because they learn best through listening and discussing, you will want to ensure you give them time to speak and to process what they hear you say.
4. Give them information in sequence as they like order and need to be able to follow a train of thought.
5. Minimize sound distractions. Make sure you coach where you won't be interrupted by the noise of colleagues outside.

6. Match their eye contact. Remember they won't make as much eye contact as a Visual, and that's perfectly fine.
7. Stand or sit close to them so that they can hear you clearly.

KINESTHETIC

The Kinesthetic individual processes the world around them through their feelings and emotions. I am most certainly a Kinesthetic, and you will often know how I am feeling just by looking at me (i.e., I flush/blush when I feel passionate about a subject I am talking about). You can see how I am feeling based on changes in my skin color. I joke that I have a magical ability to change color just based on my thoughts.

The Kinesthetic is very attached or associated with their emotions and can find it challenging to detach from them. They feel how you feel and absorb the emotions of others very quickly. When interacting with the Kinesthetic, they are likely to position their head and chin downwards. They breathe deeply from the diaphragm area and speak with a low tonality and slow tempo. Their conversation is peppered with pauses and filler words like "ummmm" and "aaahhhh," which they use to give themselves time to process their feelings before responding. There is less eye contact than from a Visual, and they will often look downwards when processing their thoughts.

They use sensory words like feel, touch, hold, and handle. You will hear them using phrases like:

- I will get in touch with you.
- I feel it in my bones.
- There was tension in the air.
- He is a warm-hearted man.
- The pressure was tremendous.
- He got the sharp end of her tongue.
- The project is up and running.
- That feels like X.
- How do you feel about that?
- Just the thought of it makes the hairs stand up on the back of my neck.
- I really want to get a handle on this and ensure I've grasped the concepts.

Other sensory words that they will use are:

Active, bearable, charge, concrete, emotional, feel, firm, flow, grasp, grip, hanging, hassle, heated, hold, hunch, pressure, solid, stir, support, tension, touch, tied, sore, hustle, rough, emotional.

Their gestures tend to be emotional and localized around the upper body. They also prefer to stand close to people and like to touch (to feel the information). The Kinesthetic is easily identifiable as the person who frequently pats you on the back, loves to give hugs, and reassures through touch. If they can't touch you, you will often see them rubbing their hands/arms/legs and the furniture around them.

The kinesthetic person's appearance is all about comfort. Rather than dressing for color coordination and neatness like the Visual, they dress for comfort. They also learn best through physical involvement, exercises, and practice. They learn through doing rather than seeing or hearing.

To best create rapport with Kinesthetics you should:

1. Give them hands-on experiences through practical exercises.
2. Give them something to touch like a printed handout, a book, or report.
3. Use Kinesthetic descriptive words.
4. Allow them to express how they feel.
5. Slow down your talking.
6. Minimize physical distractions like an uncomfortable seat or room temperature that is too hot or cold.
7. Match their eye contact.
8. Gradually sit or stand closer.

AUDITORY DIGITAL

The Auditory Digital person can often be difficult to identify as they may show signs from all the other mental maps. They prefer working with information and data. They memorize by creating steps, systems, and procedures. They may sometimes struggle to interact socially and come across as obstinate about their ideas because they are highly logic-driven. They can find it difficult to understand anybody who is not as logical as they are.

You will know an auditory digital person when they use words like:

Aware, believe, change, consider, conceive, create, decide, deliberate, develop, distinct, experience, function, indicate, know, learn, manage, motivate, opinion, plan, prepare, process, repeat, sense, think, understand, wonder.

Regarding nonverbal body language, they will engage in minimal eye contact and can sometimes seem to look right through you when they are deep in thought. They use few gestures, but you can often notice them move their lips when they are thinking—a little insight into the conversation they are having with themselves.

This internal dialogue is a key characteristic of someone with an Auditory Digital preference. When considering anything they will have an extensive internal conversation so much so it is like there is another person with them. This dialogue is important in their decision-making and communication processes. To interrupt them whilst this dialogue is happening is equivalent to interrupting two people talking and it won't be received too well!

Other characteristics are that they keep a physical distance to disconnect and analyze things, and they tend to be disassociated from their experiences. Their greatest challenge, in fact, is external sensory awareness.

You will hear them use phrases like:

- If you could describe it in more detail, I'm sure I could make sense of it.
- I need to process what we've just experienced to fully make sense of it.
- If you're sensitive to the changes in another person, you'll gain a distinct appreciation of their individual thought processes.

To create rapport with the Auditory Digital you can:

1. Use Digital descriptive words.
2. Help them learn best through reading and analysis—the more detailed, the better.
3. Make sure you're prepared and send them data to read in advance of your meeting.
4. Match their speaking tone.
5. Give them the details first.

6. Encourage them to describe what they are thinking.
7. Give them space and time to think.
8. Do not interrupt their internal dialogue.
9. Interact at their pace.

Coaching Guidelines

NOTHING IS EVER AS IT SEEMS

One of the elements of coaching that I love the most, and it hasn't changed since I started coaching many moons ago, is that nothing is ever as it seems. In 99% of coaching sessions, the initial goal or problem that the coachee says they want to address at the start of the coaching session is NEVER what we end up focusing on.

You see, for many people, a coaching session will be the first time they have been asked powerful questions about their goal, and these powerful questions serve to uncover or peel back layers of limiting beliefs and behavioral patterns that they will most likely not have been consciously aware of up until the point of coaching.

I approach every coaching session with an entirely open mind. I suspend all judgment, and my only focus is my coachee. I approach the session with a mindset of curiosity, comfortable in knowing that my coachee may not yet know the real reason behind why they want to be coached or the actual problem/opportunity they want to address.

As a coach, the worst thing you can do is to totally be guided by what your coachee says they want to focus on. Your job is to ask questions to uncover the real goal, and you use your active listening skills to ensure your client is entirely congruent about their goals.

We will cover the GROW coaching model later in the book, and there you will learn the questions you can ask to ensure your coachee is focused on the best goal for them.

BE CURIOUS

Curiosity may have killed the cat, but it is one of the main characteristics of a great coach. My coaching training has helped me recover a childlike curiosity that I thought I had lost. If you have kids, you'll be used to all those "why" questions . . . "But why is it like that?" Kids learn by being curious because it is a very effective form of learning. As a coach, you need to access that level of curiosity with your coachee. The benchmark that I use when being curious is to keep asking questions until your coachee reacts. That reaction may be surprise, sadness, confusion, or frustration. It doesn't really matter. What matters is that you've hit on something new, and now you get curious about that.

Being curious is a great frame of mind to have, and I find it can also be a lot of fun. So please don't overthink it too much. Use the questions that you will learn in the GROW model as a guide and trust your instincts. When you want the coachee to expand further (without leading them), you can say things like "Tell me more about X" or "What's X like?" or just a simple "And?"

The keys to coaching curiosity are to:

- Keep an open mind and suspend all judgment.
- Be patient and keep asking questions.
- Make no assumptions.
- Be fully present—listen like your life depends on it.
- Practice your sensory acuity.

BE A MIRROR

A mirror is a very powerful object. Sometimes we like what we see in the mirror, and sometimes we don't. Part of the role of the coach is to be a mirror for the coachee. You can do this by bringing things they say, do, and feel to their awareness. Replay what you are seeing, hearing, and feeling to them. We often get so caught up inside our heads that we lose perspective, and it can be very insightful for a coachee to get feedback on what they are projecting to the outside world.

Eric Schmidt, the Chairman of Google, has said that he believes everyone should have a coach primarily for the value you get from having a clearer perspective of yourself. We all have our blind spots, and it is incredibly difficult at times to get a clear picture of how you are perceived by your boss, your colleagues, your team, etc. Holding a mirror to ourselves is a powerful exercise to be more self-aware and in tune with how we are perceived.

Self-awareness is a key attribute of successful leaders, and by coaching your team in this way, you will dramatically increase their own self-awareness. When I want to bring something to a coachee's attention, I always ask their permission first. (E.g., "I have been noticing a particular pattern when you speak about X. Would you mind if I share it with you? I think it could be useful for you.") I have never received a "no" response to that question. We are all curious about ourselves and want to understand ourselves. I have worked in over twenty countries, and the desire for self-understanding and self-discovery is universal. We crave feedback that helps us understand ourselves better.

Here is an example of a workplace coaching conversation that I had with a young man who wanted to set some goals around his professional development, specifically in improving his emotional intelligence. At this point, we had been talking for about 20 minutes about his goal—why it was important, what it would give him, etc., and I had started to notice a pattern that I wanted to bring to his attention.

Dee: *I have been noticing a particular pattern when you speak about emotional intelligence. Would you mind if I share it with you?*

Coachee: *Sure, tell me.*

Dee: *I've noticed that whenever you say the phrase "emotional intelligence," you grimace slightly. You scrunch up your nose like you've smelled something bad.*

Coachee: *(Laughs) I don't really, do I?*

Dee: *Yes, you do. Pretty consistently as well.*

Coachee: *Oh no, that's awful.*

Dee: *What's that about?*

Coachee: *I can't believe I'm going to say this, but I actually don't want to improve my emotional intelligence.*

Dee: *What do you mean specifically?*

Coachee: *Well, if I'm perfectly honest, I've been told by my boss that I need to improve my emotional intelligence, but I don't think I do. And he totally lacks any emotional intelligence, so I don't know why he thinks I need it.*

Dee: *Okay, keep going.*

Coachee: *My team like me a lot. My employee engagement scores are amongst the highest in the company, and frankly, I am really disappointed that my boss would even think that I need to work on them.*

Dee: *Okay, I understand. So where do you think your boss might be coming from on this?*

Coachee: *I really don't know. When he told me I needed to develop my emotional intelligence, I just stayed quiet because I was too angry to talk.*

Dee: *So, you didn't disagree with him or voice a concern?*

Coachee: *No.*

Dee: *(long pause)*

Coachee: *I know what you're going to say next, Dee.*

Dee: *Okay, mind reader, tell me what I am going to say.*

Coachee: *That I should talk to my boss about it and get some more feedback.*

Dee: *Well, do you think that would be a good idea?*

Coachee: *I suppose so.*

Dee: *You suppose so?*

Coachee: *Okay, okay! Yes, it would make a lot of sense to clear the air and find out what he's thinking, and I would feel better after talking to him.*

The coachee did go speak to his boss, and his boss clarified that he specifically wanted him to focus on developing his relationships with his senior peers, and not specifically his team, because he felt that he could improve those relationships. This is where the meaning we give to words or phrases can be so unique to the speaker. When his boss said, "emotional intelligence," he was speaking about relationships with senior colleagues, whereas to the coachee it meant relationships with his team. A big difference!

This is a great illustration of how mirroring what you see and hear can uncover so much information. It would have been fruitless to work with this employee on developing his emotional intelligence when he really hadn't bought into the goal at all, and with the mirroring technique, we uncovered his resistance to the goal and found an alternative way forward.

SUSPEND ALL JUDGMENT

There is no place for judgment of any kind in coaching, and often that can be easier said than done. As a coach, your responsibility is to keep an entirely open mind about the coachee and the situation you are assisting them with. If at any time, you find yourself thinking about why they have done/said something or why they have found themselves where they are, then you are judging, and you need to stop. Go back to your curious mindset. Listen and ask a question.

You will cultivate this skill over time. We are hardwired to judge, analyze, and criticize people and situations around us all the time. The conscious part of our mind is the part of our mind we're most familiar with. It judges, evaluates, and analyzes just about everything we run across in this world, so totally suspending judgment can be a chore. And it can be done.

When working with new coaches, they frequently say the hardest part of the coaching experience for them is stopping themselves from giving advice to the coachee. The new coach believes that they know what the coachee should do to solve their problem or achieve their goal, but this is never true. And as soon as you believe you know what action the coachee should take, you have made a judgment call, and also you haven't been actively listening to the coachee if you have been busy coming up with solutions in your head!

Although in workplace coaching, you may at times give advice based on the context and the coachee; more often than not, you will be coaching so that the individual comes up with their own answers, finds their own solutions, and solves their own problems—because they can. Judging your coachee only interferes with the coaching process, and it degrades the learning experience for the coachee.

You just need to be aware of your thoughts while coaching, and as soon as you find yourself going into solution or judgment mode, refocus your energy back on the coachee.

CHECK FOR MEANING

We already have had the example of the manager and team member having different interpretations of the phrase "emotional intelligence" and the confusion that this caused. It is so important that we don't make assumptions about what people mean, particularly when they use adjectives to describe their feelings, a situation, other people, etc. For example, if I were to say that I feel very frustrated about the situation, it would be important to check what "frustrated" means specifically to me because it could mean something else to the coach. To be frustrated may mean to me that I don't like the lack of control that I have over the situation which is entirely different to feeling stressed or annoyed about the situation. Always be curious about the words people use to describe themselves and their situations. These words will be laden with meaning that can easily be missed if you don't dig a little bit deeper.

The simplest way to check for meaning is to ask the question "What does X mean to you?" So, if the coachee says they want to be happy in work, you would ask, "What does happy mean to you?" When we talked about not making judgments in the last section, this also pertained to the language people use. You want to maintain a level of curiosity about the language that your coachee is using and not judge or assume you know exactly what they mean. Checking for meaning can lift the lid on so much information for you and the coachee.

The coaching conversation is extremely unique and, when done well, it is a real journey of self-discovery for the coachee. In today's world, we don't have very deep conversations, sometimes not even with our own families. So, when a coachee has the opportunity to be asked really great questions by someone who is curious about them and their answers, it is a wonderful experience. When they are patiently and diligently asked questions that lead them to discover new things about themselves and they can express themselves and not be judged—well, I think you can guess what that feels like.

We all like to be listened to—really listened to. When people feel listened to, they feel valued, special, and important. And that's what our coachees deserve to feel: valued, special, and important. By checking for meaning, you don't just get more information as a coach, you also enable the coachee to shed light on themselves.

SILENCE IS GOLDEN

They say, "silence is golden," and when it comes to coaching, this is certainly true. I still have to consciously work hard at staying quiet during coaching sessions because I am a total extrovert. I move at a fast pace. I'm not detail-oriented, and I like quick progression. When I am coaching introverts and anyone I identify as an Auditory Digital profile, I remind myself to slow down and give these individuals time to process and think about the questions I ask. It can be incredibly annoying for a coachee to be interrupted by their coach when they want time to think and process.

Silence is a powerful form of communication and is not used nearly enough. I find that many people are uncomfortable sitting in silence with someone else—particularly in the workplace—and they feel the need to fill the silent space with chitchat.

We all have at least one person in our world that we can sit with in silence and not feel the need to speak because we are so comfortable with each other. There is no pressure to say anything or to make small talk. It's nice to sit and just be. Well, that is how it should be with your coachee, too. Remember in the coaching session that your coachee is your number one priority, and if you are focused on being uncomfortable with the silence then your attention is on you, not on the coachee.

And when you think about it, in coaching sessions the coachee is being asked questions they may never have been asked before. It is natural, therefore, that they would need time to process the questions, mull over their answers, and reflect on the new insights and learnings.

In today's world, I find that we undervalue silence. When someone is quiet, we judge and decide that they have nothing to say for themselves when this couldn't be further from the truth. We ALL have something to say for ourselves. When your coachee is silent, it doesn't mean they need help. It doesn't mean they don't know what to do. It doesn't mean they have nothing to say. When your coachee is silent, they are on an internal journey that you are not participating in. Millions of thoughts and ideas are running through their brains at the speed of light; more information is being processed than could ever be imagined. When your coachee is silent, they are working away to uncover insights, find solutions, question limiting beliefs, envision new possibilities, and so much more. Who is the coach to interrupt or interfere in that kind of magic?

And, while your coachee is going through this internal process they are still giving you clues as to what is going on inside them. Use your sensory acuity and notice eye movements—still noticeable when the coachee has their eyes closed. Changes in skin color, lip movements, head movements, and so on. There is a lot to be learned in silence, for both the coach and the coachee.

ACTIVELY LISTEN

"Listen like your life depends on it" is one of my favorite phrases, and it is what I ask my coaches to practice when they are coaching. To listen with not just their ears, but their eyes and their emotions. I recently saw one of the most perfect examples of active listening that I have ever witnessed, and it was with a young couple that was totally and absolutely head over heels in love. Yep, it was a sight to behold.

When either of them spoke, the other was totally and utterly engaged in every single word the other had to say. Eye contact was never lost, and if anything, they were lost in each other's eyes. They each showed so much interest in what the other had to say, and they asked each other great questions as if they were just delighted to learn something new about their loved one. You could see them taking in every single detail on the other's face. Total focus. Their body language was entirely in sync. When one leaned in, the other leaned in. When one moved a hand, the other moved a hand. Perfect, unconscious synchronicity. They were wrapped in a love bubble where only the two of them existed, and their only desire was to focus on the other.

Imagine being listened to like that!

Now, I'm not asking you to gaze at your coachee as if they were a love interest. That would just be creepy and inappropriate, but there is something to that total attention, curiosity, and focus that the young couple displayed. Active listening isn't just another buzzword of the day. It has existed in the world for a very long time, just in different guises. In the context of workplace coaching, it means listening with every part of your body (using your sensory acuity) and giving 110% of your focus and attention to your coachee.

You can show that you are actively listening by:

- Paying attention
- Showing you are listening through head nods
- Providing feedback through powerful questions
- By keeping an open mind
- Not interrupting
- Waiting for pauses to ask questions
- Asking questions to understand
- Paying attention to what is not being said
- Clarifying understanding
- Deferring judgment
- Responding appropriately
- Matching body language and eye contact
- Remaining curious
- Embracing silence and allowing time to think/reflect.

BE QUIETLY CONFIDENT

The focus of the coaching session is the coachee, not the coach. If for any reason you are nervous, agitated, or unfocused—whatever the case may be—then you are bringing your emotional baggage into the coaching session and you will not be able to be there for the coachee, which is your primary responsibility. Do whatever you need to do to get into the right frame of mind for a high-quality coaching session. For me, that means being entirely and totally calm, totally open, and totally present.

Nerves are completely natural especially if you are new to coaching, but again, if you are focused on your nerves, who are you not focused on? That's right, the coachee.

Remind yourself that the coaching experience is a pleasurable one. Your coachee will already be delighted just to get to spend time with you, be asked great questions, receive meaningful feedback, and learn something new about themselves. Your coaching confidence will grow as you practice and gain more experience.

And really, what's the worst that can happen? (That's another great coaching question!)

DON'T INTERRUPT

Nobody likes to be interrupted when they are thinking or speaking, right? And while we can get away with it with our families, friends, and colleagues, the coach absolutely cannot. When you interrupt a coachee, you risk breaking rapport with them, which will detract from the coaching experience and the potential outcomes. I can't stand being interrupted, and it puts me in a bad mood when I am. Imagine you are being coached, and you have just been asked this amazing, powerful question. You want time to think about it, but the coach keeps asking more questions. It's annoying.

This links back to embracing silence and giving your coachee the space to think and reflect. It is brilliant to be enthusiastic with your questions and to want to put all your new coaching skills to practice, and it is also important to respect your coachee's process. There is plenty of time, an infinite amount of time actually, so you can relax. You will be able to ask all the questions you want.

Just make it a rule not to interrupt. This will ensure the best learning experience for your coachee.

CHALLENGE

Coaching, for the most part, is not always what I would describe as a gentle process. It's a process where transformation happens, and that may not always be easy. And your coachee may not willingly embrace the change that they need. As a coach, your job is to make sure that the person has the experience that they NEED rather than the one they WANT—the one they require for transformation. That means that you will have to be comfortable and able to apply pressure at the right time and in the right areas. An example of that would be bringing to someone's attention their lack of commitment to a goal.

Let's take the scenario that someone is saying they want to be promoted, and during coaching, it has been agreed that they would work on a particular skill, like improving how they handle pressure. You still see them getting stressed out, yet they feel they are making improvements. Your job is to be totally honest with your coachee, particularly when they are not viewing the reality of their situation objectively. You cannot allow your coachee to hide from the truth. You have to bring the reality of the situation or their behavior to their attention in the most meaningful and resourceful way.

You can do that by using your questioning skills:

- What could you do differently?
- Is there anything else that you could be doing to have an even better result?
- What else do you think you need to do?

And particularly if they are avoiding the facts, maybe:
Do you mind if I bring something to your attention?

There is a way to challenge someone respectfully and politely. You don't want to go in for the kill and have an adverse reaction. You must always keep in mind the level of rapport you have with that person. Some coachees I know I can challenge directly, and they love that approach. In fact, I have some clients who specifically tell me they want me to apply a lot of pressure because they are aware of their limiting beliefs and patterns of behavior, and they know that being challenged in a direct and no-nonsense way will help them get the results they want.

We will cover this in the pre-coaching session preparation section, but a trick here is to agree to some rules prior to coaching your employee. Those rules can relate to how you will give each other feedback, what coaching style works well for them, and how they would like to receive feedback or be challenged when you believe this is necessary for them to achieve their goals. It is great to get the answers to these questions upfront, as it helps avoid confusion or stress on either party as the coaching journey gets into full swing.

From my own coaching experience, I have never had to directly challenge a coachee head-on because more often than not they have signed up to coaching because they want to achieve results and are ready to do the necessary work that it takes to achieve them. That might not always be the case in the workplace where you are coaching team members who are not voluntarily signing up to the coaching process. However, when I see someone avoiding an answer, procrastinating, or behaving in a way that does not support the achievement of their goals, I absolutely bring it to their attention, and I do not waiver until I receive a satisfactory, congruent, and authentic response.

I believe that the role of the coach is to mirror the best version of the coachee. By asking tough questions, by only accepting the best from them, and by insisting that agreed goals will be achieved, I indirectly become a model of who the coachee wants to be. I also believe that the coach needs to be strong when the coachees are not feeling strong themselves. You become strong for them until they get there themselves. This might be as simple as saying "I know you can do this" or "You're on the right track. You know you are." In tougher sessions, I have asked, in a not particularly nice tone, "Do you want to give up?" I have a 100% track record of "no" responses to that question. But sometimes you will need to ask the difficult questions, the questions no one else will ask, because as a coach, that's your job.

By my nature, I have never been a person who is comfortable with conflict, and challenging coachees was a real struggle for me at the outset. I believed that to challenge people was rude, insensitive, and not helpful. I was wrong. That was my baggage—a limiting belief. I have discovered that people are hugely resourceful, and when given an opportunity to rise to the occasion, they will take it every time. I had forgotten that I love to be challenged. It motivates me, spurs me on, and helps me reach new heights. Our coachees are the same. Challenge them and watch them rise.

GIVE NO ADVICE

Without a doubt, giving no advice was the hardest coaching skill for me to learn. I always thought my ability to give advice helped me stand out. I believed that to be a good leader I must be able to give good advice, and I worked very hard to do exactly that.

It wasn't until I began my coaching studies that I realized giving advice was not an exceptional leadership behavior, and when I thought about it, I had to admit that I never actually listened to advice that was given to me, even when I have sought it out. (And I still don't.) I realized that when I have asked for advice, it has been for the purpose of validating a decision I have already made rather than gathering alternative points of view.

When I started to practice not giving advice, initially I had to bite my tongue, so ingrained was this behavior. I also quickly realized that my desire to give advice was quite tightly tied up with my ego. Giving advice made me feel good, valued, and important. Not easy feelings to give up.

And coaching, or the role of a coach, is a great lesson in putting your ego in check and focusing all your attention on the individual you are coaching because they are the most important person in this conversation. Their outcomes and goals outrank any outcome or desire you have as a coach. Your job as a coach is to put yourself firmly out of the picture so that your full focus is on them.

If I am conducting non-workplace coaching, I stick rigidly to not giving advice, as this is the best strategy for my coaching clients. However, with workplace coaching, I have tailored that approach. I would estimate that in 80% of my workplace coaching, I apply the "no advice rule" because I want my team to be resourceful, solution-oriented, confident, empowered, and self-sustaining. If I were to answer every question for them, what would they learn? What would they do if I left the company? How is that setting them up for success? It's not!

You have to use your common sense in these cases. If you have a team member who is brand-new and doesn't know how to use a piece of software, you're not going to ask them "Well, how do you think you might use it?" That wouldn't make sense at all. You would show them how to use it, and then have them do it on their own. The same goes for decisions that need to be made quickly or may seriously impact a customer or the organization.

However, when it comes to topics like performance, career planning, and professional and personal development, I urge you to use the no advice rule at least 80% of the time. Your team members are accountable for their performance, and their career planning/development is ultimately their responsibility. They need to take responsibility for that, and that means finding their own solutions, setting their own goals, creating their plans, and taking action. You cannot do this for them, as a coach or as a manager.

NOTE TAKING

I personally do not take notes during my coaching session because I cannot have 100% full attention on my coachee when I have my head down writing notes. You can miss an incredible amount of information when you are not paying attention to the coachee, even for just a few seconds.

I find if you are actively listening, there is no need at all for notes, and note-taking can be off-putting for the coachee in that it can be distracting and the coachee may wonder and be worried about what you are writing down. Therefore, it's easier to take no notes at all.

If I feel it's necessary, I will jot down a few notes after the coaching session to ensure I capture any agreements or actions we may need to come back to at the next coaching session. In general, I will have the coachee take some notes at the end of the session because they are accountable for taking action on what has been agreed upon.

Beliefs for Professional Excellence

There are many beliefs that successful people hold that play a big part in their success. These beliefs are generally empowering, positive, goal-oriented, and enable the individual to achieve great things. They are often simple beliefs like "I will be successful," "I have the capabilities to do this," "I can learn what I don't know," "I am worthy of success," "My future is bright," etc. You will remember from the section on the Logical Levels of Learning that our behaviors are underpinned by our beliefs and values. So, from the outside, you may see a successful person and believe that it was their hard work, their discipline, and their tenacity (all the stuff that you can see) that got them to the top, and that is partially true. However, the beliefs that underpin those behaviors are equally if not more important, and these beliefs are not always visible to the outside world.

There are three beliefs that I live my life by, and they have served me, and continue to serve me very well. I teach them to my teams, and I discuss this with my coachees as I believe they are empowering beliefs that will assist them to achieve their goals. The three beliefs are:

1. There is no such thing as failure, only feedback.
2. You already have all the resources you need to solve all your problems.
3. There is a solution to every problem.

I have included them in this book because when I discuss these beliefs with my coachees, they respond to them very positively, and when things get difficult, as they sometimes do, these beliefs are an effective way of ensuring your coachee continues to take action and move forward even when they are not yet getting the results they want.

There is no such thing as failure, only feedback

Just imagine if everyone held the belief that there was no such thing as failure, only feedback. Oh, the new inventions, innovations, dreams and goals that would spring to life. Unfortunately, many of us give up on our way to achieving our goals and dreams. We give up because we don't get the results we want quickly enough or because it's just harder than we thought it was going to be. Or life gets in the way and other priorities take over. The list of reasons (or excuses) is endless.

Think of a goal that you have for yourself that you have not yet achieved despite several attempts. And consider for a moment that the world has been giving you feedback all along, and that feedback has come based on the results or lack of results that you have achieved so far. So, what do you need to do differently to get what you want? If you could tweak your approach in order to improve your chances, what tweak would you make?

They say the definition of insanity is doing the same thing over and over again and expecting different results. Based on that definition, I know a lot of totally insane people! I see it every single day—friends and colleagues working towards their dreams, applying the same approach over and over again and expecting different results, like consistency alone will be enough to get them where they need to go. If only that were true.

When you believe there is no such thing as failure only feedback, you look at everything as a lesson. When you don't get the results you want, you look for the lesson. When you get critical feedback, you look for the lesson. When you fail dismally, you look for the lesson. When your actions lead you somewhere you absolutely did not want to go, you look for the lesson.

I wish I could count the number of lessons I have had in my life, and I am quite sure I have many ahead of me still. If I did not hold this belief, I am positive I would not be where I am today. If I did not hold this belief, I would have given up on my dream of becoming an author and entrepreneur a very long time ago because I've been knocked down, and knocked down, and knocked down again. It has been a hard road, and plenty of times, I could have been forgiven for giving up, but I didn't.

Why didn't I?

Because I believe the results that I was getting were lessons, lessons that said, "Good try, now try something else," and when I could find a sense of humor about the situation, it would be more "Well, you failed spectacularly. That was fun for someone to watch. Now what will you do spectacularly next?" I absolutely believe that we are being taught lessons all the time. Some lessons we notice, and some we don't. Let me give you an example:

That person at work that you don't get on with at all, the one that really gets on your nerves, he/she is teaching you a lesson. They may not know it, but they are. If you think about that person for a moment, what lesson does that person have for you? What can you learn from your interaction with them? When I posed this same question to myself, my answer surprised me, and it was that the individual was not intentionally trying to annoy me. They were trying, however, to get something important from me, and actually, I was the one making it difficult for them. Why was I making it difficult for them? I felt a need to exert power. The individual was a typical dominant alpha male, and I was responding very out of character because I felt intimidated, and I did not like feeling that way. My lesson—communicate in a new way with this person to find a win-win solution.

Now, I could have easily ignored the lesson and carried on with the dysfunctional relationship, but what good would that do? And your coachees have the option to ignore the lessons that are waiting to be learned, but what good would that do, too? The important takeaway here is that failure is optional, and it's a choice, which places it in your control. When you choose as a coach to believe that there is no such thing as failure, only feedback, you will be a phenomenal coach and will have a lifelong journey of learning. When you encourage your coachees to hold this belief, you instill in them a powerful belief which they can rely on when times get tough and a belief that will hold them accountable for their choices, actions, and behavior.

You already have all the resources you need to solve all of your problems

Everything a person needs to effect change in their lives is already in them. The most basic resource we all have is the ability to learn.

The resources that this belief is describing is one's inner resources. For example, confidence, patience, humor, perspective, discipline, and persistence. This is one of my favorite beliefs because it is empowering, and when taken on by a coachee, it leads to high levels of personal accountability, ownership, and commitment. If you truly believe that you have all the resources you need to solve all of your problems, then there is no place for excuses.

I recently coached a senior manager who was feeling powerless about achieving the personal development goal of becoming more inspirational, specifically in his leadership style. We discussed what resources he already had that could be considered inspirational outside the office environment. He mentioned that he coached his son's football team, and he felt inspiring in that role and had feedback from their parents to that very point. We were able to break down what made him inspiring as a football coach and how he could leverage those resources in the office. We came up with a list of resources he already had like:

1. Energetic
2. Sense of humor
3. Passionate
4. Ambitious
5. Goal-oriented
6. Belief in the team
7. Caring
8. Has a game plan
9. Celebrates success and failure
10. Learns from mistakes.

We followed this up with a discussion on how he could apply each of these resources to his corporate leadership style and how he was going to take action to immediately leverage these skills. He is well on his way to being one of the most inspirational leaders in his organization.

The key point in this belief is that all the resources you need to become or do whatever it is that you want to do are deep within you. The challenge is to look for and make effective use of those resources when you need to. When coaching, I always work with my coachees to identify all the resources they have available to them—both internal and external—that they can access whenever they need.

There is no such thing as unresourceful people, just unresourceful states of mind. It is also important to note that asking for help is a resourceful skill that all of us possess. Many of us believe that asking for help is a sign of weakness when it is really a sign of strength. Is that a belief that you might hold yourself? And if it is, who said we have to do everything all by ourselves? If someone asked you for help would you be there for them? What makes you think that someone might not be there for you?

There is a solution to every problem

There is a solution to every problem, and if you genuinely hold this belief, there is an increased likelihood that you will find the solution. People who uncover solutions to problems are those who are confident that the solutions do indeed exist. They just haven't found them yet.

Holding this belief has meant that I never give up when it comes to things that are important to me. My entrepreneurial journey has been interesting, to say the least. I have made some spectacular mistakes, and I have had great successes. With the parts of the journey I've got wrong, I inherently believe that there is a solution out there. I just haven't uncovered it yet. And with this mindset, I persist in finding the solution by using all the resources I have at my disposal. The definition of insanity is doing the same thing over and over again while expecting different results. When applying this belief, I am continuously tweaking my approach until I get the result that I want.

When I have been stuck and completely dumbfounded as to how to proceed, I have used my external as well as my internal resources to keep me moving forward. Those external resources can be other coaches, mentors, friends, and family. I will often look for role models who have faced and overcome the type of problem that is facing me so that I can model and learn what worked successfully for them.

Interestingly, I was recently coaching a senior executive who had reached a roadblock in her development. Her goal was to speak on a TedTalk. This goal was paramount to her and something she had dreamed of achieving for a long time. She had been studying online resources about how to put together a successful talk, and she was confident in reaching this part of the goal. Where she was struggling was getting the invitation to speak. I have known this particular leader for quite some time. She is very independent, a creative problem solver; however, I know that she prefers to solve problems on her own. She has a limiting belief that asking for help makes her look weak.

I asked her if she knew anybody else who had presented at a TedTalk, and she said, "Yes, I know three people who have done it, and they were really good." So, you can probably guess my next question. "Have you spoken to them about how they got their invitations?" She hesitated before responding, "No, I have not." I proceeded and asked, "What is stopping you from contacting them?" and she said she would prefer to arrange it on her own. Now because I have been coaching this person for quite a while, and we had discussed her limiting belief about asking for help, I went with a more direct line of questioning:

Dee: *If you could choose to do the TedTalk next week or next year, which would you choose?*

Leader: *Next week of course.*

Dee: *How long have you been working on getting this TedTalk together?*

Leader: *Oh, about three months.*

Dee: *How is your approach working out for you?*

Leader: *(long pause) It's taking longer than I would like.*

Dee: *How do you feel about that?*

Leader: *I am starting to feel frustrated, . . . like it might never happen.*

Dee: *What are you going to do differently to get the result you want?*

Leader: *(long pause) I can call one of my friends who has done a TedTalk before.*

Dee: *Okay, when are you going to do that?*

Leader: *I'll call him tomorrow.*

Dee: *What's stopping you from making the call right now?*

Leader: *Nothing.*

Dee: *So, make the call.*

She did make the call, which resulted in her being introduced to one of the people who books speakers for TedTalks, and she is now scheduled to speak in July 2017.

The problems and challenges we experience in our lives significantly contribute to the learning process of successfully solving problems and achieving our goals. In fact, many successful people admit that they view every problem as an opportunity. It all depends on one's perception.

If you concentrate hard on finding a solution to a problem and you sincerely believe you will find it, you will get it sooner or later. Your thinking makes a world of difference to the kind of result you can expect to achieve when faced with a problem.

Build Your Self-Awareness

The Johari window is an easy way of assessing your self-awareness and the awareness that others have about you. It is designed to reveal what you know or do not know about yourself. It also uncovers what you reveal to others and what others know about you without you being aware of it.

The larger the OPEN plane in your Johari window (known by you and by others), the more likely others are to know and understand you. The more transparent you are, the more likely people will interact with you in an honest and open fashion.

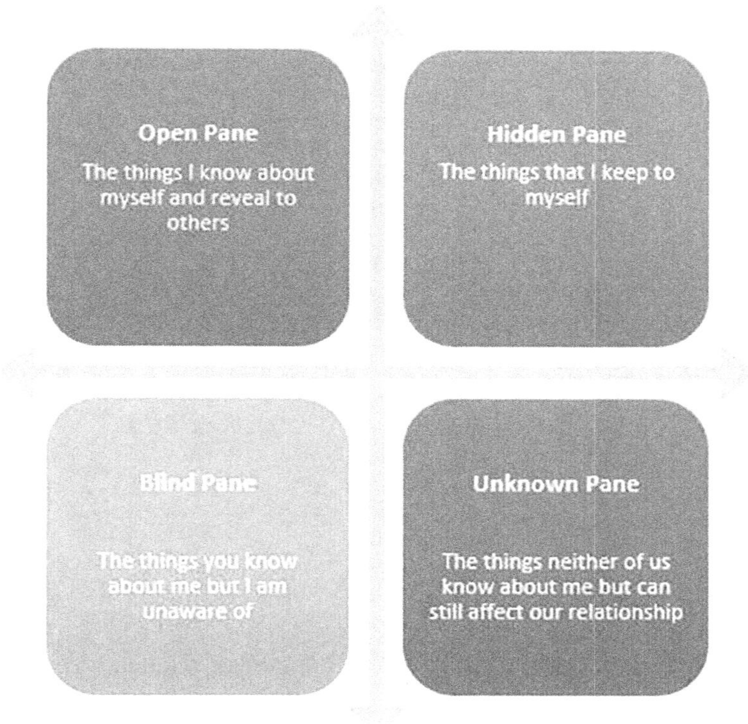

The quadrants in the Johari window are shown as equal in size when, in fact, the relative size of each pane can vary between individuals. For example, a very private or introverted person might always maintain a slender OPEN pane, and conversely, a strong extrovert will gladly share lots of information about themselves (even when not directly asked).

This is a fantastic coaching exercise when you want to cultivate self-awareness. We all have our blind spots; however, to be successful in the workplace, we all must become more aware of these blind spots so that they don't hold us back. I suggest that you try out this exercise right now because the best coaches and leaders I have worked with are highly self-aware. You can then use it with your coachees to develop their own self-awareness.

Using the following Johari window, follow these instructions:

1. In the Open quadrant (top left), write down what is known by you and by others.
2. In the Hidden quadrant (top right), write down what is known by you and not known by others.
3. In the Blind quadrant (bottom left), write down what is not known by you but known by others. You will need to ask others for this feedback.
4. In the Unknown pane (bottom right), write down what may not be known by anyone but could affect a relationship.

OPEN Pane Known by both of us	HIDDEN Pane Known only to me
The open area reflects the "open book" of ourselves: our attitudes, behavior, motivation, values, and way of life. Record here the knowledge that you and others have of you. Expand this pane as you disclose and learn more.	The degree to which we share ourselves with others (disclosure) is the degree to which we can be known. Record here what you freely keep to yourself. Ask yourself whether sharing that knowledge will benefit your relationships.
BLIND Pane Known to YOU but not to ME	**UNKNOWN Pane Unknown to both of us**
When others provide feedback in a supportive, responsible way, and you can take it in that way, you are able to test the reality of who you are and grow in self-awareness. Record here feedback that has given you useful insights.	Be open to experiences that seem to reveal something from your subconscious like feelings, reading, listening, and dreaming. Record here chance experiences.

Once you have completed this exercise, ask yourself the following questions:

- What feedback would I like to receive in order to understand where I can develop?
- From whom should I receive this feedback?

How to Set Powerful Goals

Coaching is goal- and action-oriented so it is crucial that the workplace coach can assist their coachee to comprehensively articulate and document their desired goals. Many of you will already be familiar with the SMART goal model as this is most commonly used in business. In the SMART model goals should be:

- Specific
- Measurable
- Achievable
- Relevant
- Time-bound

The goal model I have outlined below takes SMART much further and incorporates the most recent research and best practice in goal setting. There are nine steps to be followed in this model and there is a pre-designed template included so that you can test it out yourself.

1. Positively Stated: What exactly do you want?

Make sure your goal is stated in positive terms of what you want and not what you don't want. (E.g., instead of "I don't want to get nervous when I present," you can phrase this as "I want to be confident, calm, and in control when I present.") All goals need to be stated positively, focusing on what you want rather than what you don't want.

2. Control: Can you achieve this goal yourself, no matter what other people do?

Make sure the goal is stated in a way that you get it yourself, leaving no room for blaming other people or circumstances. (E.g., "I want to stop panicking when the audience doesn't respond to me." You have no control over the audience, do you? It is not self-maintained. You want to write it as "I will remain in a calm and resourceful state when the audience doesn't respond, and objectively use other well thought out questions to induce their involvement with me.")

3. Evidence: How will you know when you accomplished your goal?

Imagine achieving your goal now. What will you see, hear or feel? State your goal in sensory-specific details. (E.g., "I will know I've reached my goal when I feel confident" is not sensory specific. The right evidence is "When I hear senior managers asking me for an appointment after my presentation, and I hear myself answering all of their questions in a calm and confident voice, I can also see the room being filled with lively people, talking excitedly amongst themselves about my ideas.")

4. Context: Where, when, and with whom do you want it?

Under what situations do you want to use this outcome? Do you want this result all the time? With whom do you want it? When do you want that result to materialize? (E.g. "When I see myself at the top of the boardroom, and I am speaking confidently, clearly, and with power. I feel confident and in control. Everyone in the room is engaged in my presentation and giving me positive feedback.")

5. Preventing: What stops you from already having accomplished your goal?

Knowing what usually stops you from achieving your goal helps you formulate strengths to overcome it and become aware of those potential roadblocks. Some examples might be:

- I don't feel entirely confident yet.
- I need more time to practice.
- I am worried that my boss won't be satisfied with my presentation.

Note down these roadblocks and what specifically you will do to ensure that your progress does not slow down or stall.

6. Resources: What resources do you already have that will assist you in reaching your goal? What other resources do you need?

a. I have presented before, and most of those presentations have gone well. I can use these previous experiences positively.
b. I can attend a public speaking class.
c. I can get advice and feedback from my colleague who is excellent at public speaking.
d. I know my content inside out, and this gives me confidence.

7. Ecology: What might you gain or lose in achieving this goal?

Will you lose anything that you now have when you reach this goal? This means thinking about your goal in a holistic sense, including its effects on other areas of your life and how it might affect other people you care for. A typical example would be around promotion. You may have to spend less time at home or with family and friends because you will have to work late. Or you may have less time for your hobbies because more of your day will be required in the office.

We often neglect to take a holistic view of our goals, and it is important to address the parts of your life that may be adversely impacted by the achievement of a particular goal. One of the most common coaching sessions I have with new managers is the difficulty they face leading a team of people that were once their peers and friends. When the goal is the first promotion into a leadership position, we rarely think about the reaction of our colleagues and how some friendships may be lost or damaged along the way.

8. Worthwhile: What will achieving this outcome offer you? Or what is so important to you about this goal?

When we are clear about how our outcome will fulfill the important things we value, we will naturally be more motivated to do it.

9. Action: What and when is your first step in getting this goal into motion?

Achieving goals is all about taking action, and while coaching, you want to ensure your coachee is ready and motivated to take the necessary steps to move forward, even if that means baby steps. Be clear about exactly what action will be taken, when specifically, and what will happen next.

Keys to an Achievable Outcome Worksheet

Note: Some questions may be more relevant than others.

1. Positively Stated

What exactly do you want?

Pick one outcome if you have several. Which outcome, when achieved, will have the greatest impact?

I want

…………………………………………………………………………………….

…………………………………………………………………………………….

…………………………………………………………………………………….

…………………………………………………………………………………….

…………………………………………………………………………………….

2. Control (self-maintainable)

What specifically will you do to achieve this goal? Is it stated in a way that you can achieve it yourself, no matter what other people do?

I will

…………………………………………………………………………………….

…………………………………………………………………………………….

…………………………………………………………………………………….

…………………………………………………………………………………….

…………………………………………………………………………………….

3. Evidence of achieving it

a) How specifically will you know when you have achieved your outcome?
b) What are the performance criteria and how will they be tested?
c) What will be your ongoing feedback that you are moving toward or away from your goal?
   a) Ensure that your outcome is testable in sensory experience.
   b) That must have sensory evidence to prove your achievement.

I will have achieved my goal when:

……………………………………………………………………………

……………………………………………………………………………

……………………………………………………………………………

4. Context

a) When do you want to achieve this? What is a realistic time frame?
b) Under what conditions do you want/not want to implement this outcome?
c) With whom do you need/want to share this outcome?

I want to achieve this outcome by:

……………………………………………………………………

……………………………………………………………………

I want

……………………………………………………………………

……………………………………………………………………

5. Preventing

a) What stops you from already having accomplished your goal?
b) What resistance or interference have you encountered?
c) What is currently needed or missing from the plan?

……………………………………………………………………………

……………………………………………………………………………

……………………………………………………………………………

……………………………………………………………………………

……………………………………………………………………………

6. Resources

a) Have you ever been able to achieve an outcome like this before? What did you do?
b) Do you know of someone else who has been able to achieve an outcome like this before? What did this person do?
c) What (behavior, state, ability, belief, support) do you have that will help you to achieve your outcome?
d) What (behavior, state, ability, belief, support) when you get them would make the achievement of this outcome undeniable?
e) What (behavior, state, ability, belief, support) would make it impossible for this problem to continue?
f) If you did have the resources you need to achieve your outcome, what would they be?

....

....

....

....

....

....

....

7. Ecology

a) What will you gain or lose in achieving this outcome?
b) Are there any areas in your life where achieving this outcome could be disadvantageous?
c) What positive gains are there in the present ways of doing things?

....

....

………………………………………………………………………………….

………………………………………………………………………………….

8. Worthwhile (higher purpose)

a) What will achieving this outcome get for you?
b) If you achieve this outcome, what will it do for you?

If I get that, then I will:

………………………………………………………………………………….

………………………………………………………………………………….

………………………………………………………………………………….

What will achieving this outcome get for you?

If I get that, then I will:

………………………………………………………………………………….

………………………………………………………………………………….

………………………………………………………………………………….

9. Action

a) How can you break this outcome down into smaller manageable steps?
b) What will be your first step in getting this outcome into motion?
c) When will you start it?
d) What can you do now (on top of what you've already done) to bring yourself one step closer to your outcome?
e) How will you know if you are moving towards your outcome?

………………………………………………………………………………….

………………………………………………………………………………….

………………………………………………………………………………….

....

....

....

....

....

....

....

....

....

Visualization

"Everything you can imagine is real."

– Pablo Picasso

Stephen Covey, the well-known author of *The 7 Habits of Highly Effective People* said, "Develop your imagination—you can use it to create in your mind what you hope to create in your life." The use of visualizations in coaching is an amazingly effective way to bring your coachees' goals to life. They are a powerful tool that can also be used to change a person's mood or mental state in a matter of moments. Just take a moment to visualize the last time you felt totally happy, calm, and relaxed. Close your eyes and visualize that moment clearly, taking time to notice all of the details—the sounds, sights, and emotions attached to the visual. Enjoy the moment and take your time.

How did that feel? Isn't it amazing how quickly you can bring those feelings back to life? How do you feel now?

Our senses are powerful. Even a smell can bring you immediately back to a childhood memory. (For me, the smell of freshly cut grass immediately takes me back to the field in front of my parents' house.) Or maybe it's a song, a book, the taste of a particular food. Visualizations can be used as a coaching tool for many different purposes, and I want to focus on its use in assisting your coachees to achieve their goals.

It is commonplace these days to hear of top athletes using visualization as part of their peak performance approach. For example, top golf players visualizing the perfect swing and matching their practice to that visualization.

Jim Carrey

In the early 1990s, Jim Carrey was just starting out in his acting career and struggling to get by. To keep motivated, he wrote himself a check for $10 million for "acting services rendered," and dated it for 1994. He carried it with him in his wallet, to inspire and motivate himself each and every day. In 1994, he learned he would earn precisely $10 million for his lead role in *Dumb and Dumber*. Today Carrey is an internationally recognized movie star, and in interviews, he has frequently cited his visualization as being a key part of his early success.

Oprah Winfrey

The phenomenon that is Oprah Winfrey (and one of my personal role models) has well-known rags to riches story. She overcame what can only be described as an extremely challenging childhood to become one of the most successful female entrepreneurs in the world. When talking about her success, she has described using visualization from a very early age, focusing on living a very different life than the one she was born into.

If you have watched any of Oprah's television shows, you will know that she often showcases success stories of positive thinking and has even shared her own vision boards, which she regularly uses to realize her dreams. One of my favorite Oprah quotes is "Create the highest, grandest vision possible for your life because you become what you believe."

Wayne Rooney

Whether you are a Manchester United supporter or not, I think we can all agree that Wayne Rooney is a gifted player and has had an extremely successful sporting career. Rooney has revealed that prior to a match "I lie in bed the night before the game and visualize myself scoring goals or doing well." Knowing exactly what kit he will be wearing also helps him construct a more detailed, authentic and compelling visual. "I don't know if you'd call it visualizing or dreaming, but I've always done it, my whole life."

Lindsey Vonn

Lindsey is one of the most successful female skiers in history. She has frequently shared details of her mental preparation, which she cites as giving her a significant competitive edge. "I always visualize the run before I do it," Vonn told MindBodyGreen. "By the time I get to the start gate, I've run that race 100 times already in my head, picturing how I'll take the turns."

But Vonn takes her visualizations one step further by incorporating the physical simulation of her goals along with her visualizations. She does this by literally going through the motions of skiing (i.e., moving her weight from one leg to the other, simulating her breathing, etc.). "Once I visualize a course, I never forget it. So I get on those lines and go through exactly the run that I want to have."

So, what makes visualization such a powerful technique for success?

Based on research by Srinivasan Pillay, a Harvard M.D. and author of *Your Brain and Business: The Neuroscience of Great Leaders*, he explains that "we stimulate the same brain regions when we visualize an action as we do when we actually perform that same action." So, by visualizing your desired goal, to your brain, it's the same as taking the action necessary to achieve the goal—the brain does not differentiate between what is imagined and what is real. When you bring visualizations into your coaching practice, you are essentially helping your coachees to condition their brains for success. This is simply done by first deciding what the goal is then visualizing the goal in as much detail as possible—in visual, auditory, kinesthetic, and auditory digital terms. Then continue to focus on that visualization over the long term.

Now obviously for the achievement of goals, visualization alone is not enough. The coachee must take action. However, if your coachees cannot clearly picture themselves achieving their goal then there is a high likelihood that they won't achieve it. I find that including an element of visualization when setting goals helps your coachee to connect more meaningfully to the goal, gets them excited about what that goal will bring and/or how it will change their life, and can help to uncover any unconscious limiting beliefs.

When I started workplace coaching, I was nervous about including visualizations in my practice as I had a number of limiting beliefs:

1. Visualizations, as a coaching tool, are not appropriate in an office environment.
2. If I ask a coachee to go through a visualization, they'll think I'm not serious or professional, and it will damage my reputation.
3. Coachees will be uncomfortable experiencing visualizations in an office environment.

And boy, was I wrong! I learned a couple of very valuable lessons from my coachees when I started to incorporate visualizations:

1. When there is good rapport between coach and coachee, the coachee does not question the exercises the coach chooses to use as they trust the coach knows what they are doing and will only ask them to participate in exercises that will help them achieve their goals.
2. If you, as a coach, believe visualizations are "hippy" and not meant for the workplace, your coachee will pick up on this. And the opposite is true—choose to believe that your coachee will gain insight and learn from the visualization experience, and that is exactly what will happen.
3. There is no exercise that is inappropriate in an office environment as it all depends on the needs of your coachee and the level of rapport you have with them. Honestly, I have tried some pretty off-the-wall exercises during workplace coaching based solely on the fact that I knew what my coachee needed, and they benefited from the experience. Never assume what your coachee may think is weird or hippy. Have confidence in your skill set and toolkit and keep focused on the needs of your coachee.

You may also choose to have your coachee design a vision board, perhaps of their ideal career. I will often include vision board exercises in group coaching sessions, and it always goes down really well. A vision board is basically a different type of visualization, just in a physical form. You will need to do some advance preparation for a vision board exercise in the form of the materials that the coachee will need (i.e., a board or piece of card, magazines from which to cut out nice visuals, glue, stickers, tape, scissors, and so on). The task for the coachee is to get creative and use visuals from the magazines to create a vision of their goal. I also give the following instructions:

1. Think big—there are no small parts, only small actors.
2. You have permission to be greedy. This is your life. You only get to do this once!
3. Fill the page.
4. If your vision board doesn't inspire you, this is a reflection of your goals. Make it inspiring!
5. Commit to taking action and share your board with your friends, family, and colleagues.
6. Post your board somewhere you will see it every day.

Part 3:
The Coaching Session

Coaching Session Pre-work

This section includes examples of pre-work that you and your coachee can review and complete prior to the first coaching session. I use pre-work not just to find out more about the coachee in advance of coaching but also to check that they have fully bought into the process and are willing to put in and commit to the work. If someone cannot complete pre-work for me on the time that is agreed, that is a signal about their commitment to the process, and in many cases, is an early indicator of limiting beliefs.

Designing interesting and relevant pre-work is a great way to kick off your coaching. Well-considered pre-work shows your coachee that this is a process that you are serious about. It sets the tone for how the coaching will be conducted, and it communicates that their participation is critical to its success. I have included as many pre-work options as I possibly can, and it is up to you which and/or how many you choose to use. Please feel free to tailor the templates to your requirements.

COACHING AGREEMENT IN THE WORKPLACE

In workplace coaching, there needs to be a clear set of confidentiality boundaries, which are agreed upon at the outset. This may not be an issue when the coaching is between leader and team member but is definitely necessary when it is between an employee and external coach or any other individual who is not the employee's manager. Getting clear on confidentiality boundaries is important to build trust and avoid confusion later in the coaching process.

In the latest International Coaching Federation (ICF) survey, respondents were asked, "Who is kept apprised of progress?" when an employee is being coached. The responses were:

Coach:	87.9%
Manager:	67.9%
HR:	55.7%
Other:	27.1%

From my experience, the more confidentiality in coaching, the better; however, in the workplace, this may not always be possible, particularly if a third party (like HR or senior management) needs to be kept up to date on progress. This doesn't mean that every single conversation point needs to be shared, however, there may be a need to share specific information on goals, progress and feedback.

I have three rules that I use in workplace coaching that have served my coachees well. I conform to the KISS (keep it simple stupid) method of agreement design:

1. From the outset, be clear on who, other than you, will need to be kept updated on coaching progress and why it is to the benefit of the coachee that this third party is involved. (E.g., "On a monthly basis, I will provide a report to Ellen in HR. It is important that I keep Ellen informed as she is very interested in your potential and will want to specifically know about your career goals and timelines. Is that ok?")
2. Everything else in the coaching conversation is kept confidential other than what is agreed in point one. This is very important as it gives the coachee space to be able to confide in you with trust.
3. I have one disclaimer that I communicate prior to the first coaching session, and this is "Unless I have stated otherwise, this coaching session will be entirely confidential. In the interest of total disclosure, I have one disclaimer, and that is if I believe that either you or the company are at risk—for example, you are stressed out and I think your health could be adversely affected or your actions could pose a risk to the company's performance—then I will seek advice from a third party. For example, HR. That said, if I choose to take such action, I will make you aware that I am doing so. Is that ok?"

I can guarantee that your coachee will appreciate your honesty in clearly outlining the confidentiality boundaries, and this will help to build trust and rapport. In all my years of coaching, I have not yet had anyone disagree with the above terms, and thankfully, I have not yet had to invoke my disclaimer.

Exercise: Coaching Questions

I am looking forward to our first coaching session. I have seen the benefits that coaching can bring in enabling people to achieve their goals, reach their potential, change limiting beliefs and behaviors, and much more. As your manager, I am excited that you get to experience these benefits, too. In advance of our coaching session, I would like you to take some time to fill out the answers to the questions below. Coaching is a very individual process that makes it unique to you, and I want to make sure that I gain as much insight about you as I can so that this process is valuable, informative, and relevant.

I estimate that it will take approximately forty-five minutes to complete the questionnaire. I would encourage you to take your time and think through your answers. We will use your responses as a basis for discussion in our first coaching session. I would appreciate it you could email me your completed questionnaire 48 hours prior to our scheduled coaching.

If you had to describe yourself in five words, what would they be?

....

....

....

....

....

....

If there was a secret passion in your life, what would it be?

....

....

....

....

....

....

If there was a specific behavior (your own) that you would like to eliminate or change, what would it be and why?

....

....

....

....

....

....

What motivates you?

....

....

....

....

....

....

What or who inspires you?

....

....

....

....

....

....

What accomplishment are you most proud of and why?

....

....

....

....

....

....

What does success mean for you? What would a successful life look, sound, and feel like?

....

....

....

....

....

....

If you weren't working in the job you have now, what would you be doing?

....

....

....

....

....

What are your top three fears?

....

....

....

....

....

....

What do you most want to get out of coaching?

....

....

....

....

....

....

What do I need to know about you to ensure we have a successful coaching relationship?

....

....

....

....

....

....

How rigorous do you want me to be as your coach?

....

....

....

....

....

....

How do you best learn? What is your learning style?

....

....

....

....

....

....

How specifically do you release stress?

....

....

....

....

....

....

What would you most like to learn, and why?

....

....

....

....

....

....

When do you feel the most confident, and why?

....

....

....

....

....

....

What are your strengths that differentiate you most from others?

....

....

....

....

....

....

What really gets under your skin and makes you mad?

....

....

....

....

....

....

What is the most valuable life lesson you've learned so far?

....

....

....

....

....

....

How will you know this coaching has been successful?

....

....

....

....

....

....

Exercise: Wheel of Life

This exercise is called the Wheel of Life, and its purpose is to help you get a baseline of how satisfied you currently are in different areas of your life and where there may be room for improvement. It can help you plan a life that is more satisfying, and it serves to clarify priorities for goal setting during our coaching sessions.

The wheel contains eight different segments that reflect distinct areas of your life.

1. Business/Career (This might be school/college—if coaching students.)
2. Finances
3. Health
4. Family and Friends
5. Romance (This could also be marriage or personal relationships.)
6. Personal Growth
7. Fun and Recreation
8. Physical Environment (This relates to the world around us, the world we live in.)

If one or more of the segments in the wheel is not relevant to you, please feel free to relabel it. You may want to include an additional segment, and that's okay, too. Segments that you could add are Spirituality or Religion, Purpose or Values. It's completely up to you.

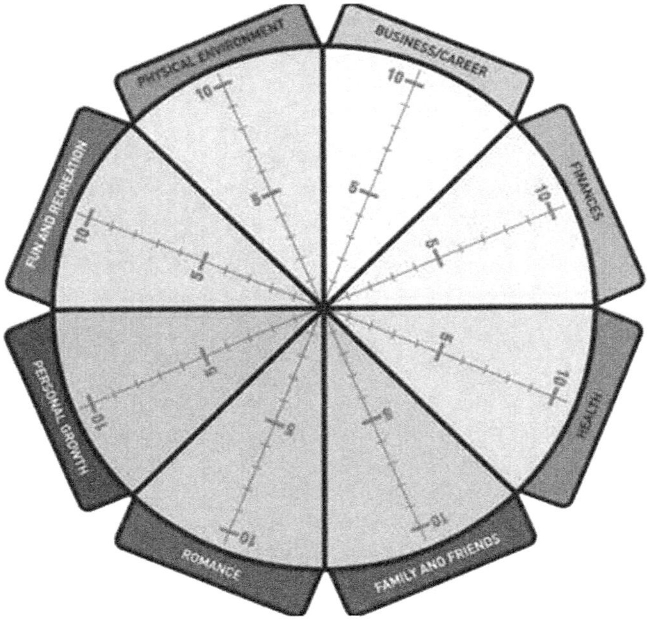

Take a moment to review each part of the wheel and consider what the ideal situation or scenario would be for that part of your life. You may choose to visualize your goals in each area, your achievements to date, and what's going well and not so well.

When you are ready, score each piece of the wheel from zero to ten —zero being totally dissatisfied and 10 being totally satisfied. Your score must reflect how you are doing in that part of your life **TODAY**, not how you would like it to be. Be honest with yourself, and there is no wrong answer! A balanced life is unique to each person. What might be satisfying or ideal for one person may be stressful or frustrating for another. It is also important to note that our preferences and priorities change over time. For example, a 16-year-old will not hold Business/Career as high a priority as a 36-year-old. The same can be said for Romance.

Once you have finished scoring your wheel, take a moment to reflect on your scores, and then answer the following questions:

How do you feel about your scores?

....

....

....

....

....

Are there any insights or surprises?

....

....

....

....

....

Which of these categories would you most like to improve?

....

....

....

....

....

What change do you want to make first?

....

....

....

....

....

What are the top three actions that you are going to take, and by when?

....

....

....

....

....

....

Is there anything stopping you from taking this action?

....

....

....

....

....

....

Building Rapport

Rapport is the most important process in any human interaction. It describes a feeling of shared understanding, a close and harmonious relationship in which the people concerned understand each other's feelings, ideas, and points of view. Without rapport, people will not trust each other, will not communicate effectively with each other, and most certainly will not be able to develop a functional relationship, either professional or personal.

We all have the ability to create rapport, and we do it multiple times every single day. Think of individuals at work that you feel most comfortable with, those that you confide in, talk to openly and feel a sense of connection to. With those people, you have high rapport. Rapport can also be created with absolute strangers. Can you remember someone you met for the first time, and you felt like you had known them forever? We've all had that kind of rapport experience, and because it manifests so effortlessly, people tend to think it just happens, when in fact, we can establish rapport in a very deliberate manner.

What is critical to understand about rapport is that it is a process, and there are very specific things you can do to establish rapport with someone. Psychologists have discovered three distinct elements to building rapport:

- Mutual attention where each party is tuned into the other
- A shared positive feeling conveyed primarily by nonverbal body language (e.g., smiles, leaning forward, head nods, etc.)
- Synchrony which is when people unconsciously respond to each other's movements and gestures.

It is human nature for us to like those who are like us whether that be based on race, gender, nationality, sexual orientation, age, hobbies, culture, educational background, political affiliations, etc. We are drawn to people who are like us. From a coaching point of view, the best way to create high levels of rapport is to become more like the other person. You want them to say to themselves, "I like you, you're like me"—at least in their heads. Why?

Because with rapport comes trust, and with trust comes a more constructive, open, honest, and ultimately successful coaching session for the coachee. It is normal that when you feel at ease with someone, you will be more relaxed and open with them. There is less reason to feel the need to be guarded or cautious of what you say.

Ultimately, if you don't have rapport, you will not get your desired outcome. This applies to any relationship. Without trust, the foundations of a relationship are destined to crumble. Luckily, you don't have to like a person to create rapport, so there is never any excuse to not build rapport even with individuals you don't like—a necessary skill in the workplace.

So, how will you know when you have rapport?

Quite simply put, you will feel it. You will feel at ease. Your coachee will be giving you signals that they are positively engaged with the interaction. Everything will be happening very fluidly. Conversely, if you don't have rapport or you lose it, you will feel uncomfortable, and even if your coachee tries to hide it, they will still show signals that they are uncomfortable, too.

You can test for rapport through matching (we go into this in the next section). Once you feel you have a good level of rapport, make a small change in your body language (e.g., move the position of your arm, cross your legs, or lean forward slightly). If rapport is there, the individual will follow your lead and match the change in your body language within about ten seconds. If this doesn't happen, continue to focus on building rapport, and make the body language change later until it is reciprocated.

When your coachee is experiencing high levels of rapport, they will often come straight out and tell you. They may say something like "I feel like I have known you for ages" or "I've never told anyone this before" or "I feel really comfortable talking to you."

There are many techniques detailed in this book to help you create the highest levels of rapport—from mirroring and matching words, the tone of voice and body language, to leading and pacing, using your sensory acuity and applying all of the coaching guidelines detailed earlier in the book.

In my opinion, your ability to build rapport is one of the key success factors to becoming a successful coach. If you cannot build trust with your coachee, then the coaching session itself will not yield results. Fortunately, you already know how to build rapport so all you need to do is fine-tune it a bit for the purposes of high-performance coaching.

MIRRORING AND MATCHING

Behavioral research shows that mirroring and matching, or copying other people's body language, mannerisms, and repeating their words does greatly help to build trust and establish rapport. Some of us create rapport quite instinctively—just think of that charismatic person in the office who genuinely gets along and is liked by everyone. Not all of us possess this ease in building rapport, but not to worry. Matching and mirroring, just like building rapport, can be learned.

First, let's take a look at the difference between mirroring and matching.

Mirroring is quite simply the process of copying or reflecting back someone's verbal and nonverbal body language. When this is done with respect and discretion, it leads to a general sense of positivity and ease between you and your coachee.

Matching, on the other hand, can have a built-in time delay. For example, if your coachee changes their seating position from leaning forward to leaning back and at the same time uncrosses their arms, you would wait about 10 seconds and then match their new seating position.

The most effective way to establish rapport quickly is to mirror and match the most unconscious elements of a person's behavior during communication. More specifically focusing on their body language and tonality, which we know makes up 93% of our communication. Paying attention to just these two communication channels is enough to powerfully build rapport in a manner that is not off-putting to the coachee and, when done well, is completely unnoticeable.

New coaches often find mirroring and matching uncomfortable as they feel like they are mimicking the person as a young child would or that they are not congruent themselves when taking on their coachee's posture and movement. However, when done properly, mirroring and matching is a very powerful way to indirectly and subtly create rapport with someone. It does not mean that you have to sit the same way they do or change your body language precisely at the moment they do. That would be really off-putting and rude.

What it means is paying attention to how the person is sitting, standing, moving, speaking, and ensuring that you are, as much as possible, in alignment with them. Remember to create rapport you want to be like the other person and that entails inhabiting their patterns, traits, and language (verbal and nonverbal).

Mirroring and matching can happen at many different levels—mirroring someone's breathing for example (speed, position, sound). Even a person's blinking rate can be matched. I would encourage you to start out just mirroring how someone sits and stands. Notice where they place their arms and hands, where their feet are positioned. Are they crossed? Under the chair? Are they sitting up straight, leaning back, or forwards?

I have found that I have been able to apply my mirroring and matching skills to better understand relationships at work, particularly when I am new to that business or client. In the next meeting you attend, look around the room and watch how people mirror and match each other without even knowing they're doing it. You can very quickly see if someone is in rapport with someone else, or the opposite—if they are literally not seeing eye to eye at all.

Mirroring and matching, like all coaching skills, has a much wider application beyond one-to-one coaching, and it will give you a real edge regarding better understanding people, relationships, and complex situations.

PACE AND SPEED

We know from reviewing the different mental map preferences—Visual, Auditory, Kinesthetic and Auditory Digital—that people often speak at a different rate. Some speak quickly like the Visuals; some more slowly like the Kinesthetics, and they use many filler words like "um." Just like the mirroring and matching of body language, tone of voice, and words, you can also mirror and match the speed, rate, or pace that someone speaks. You can do this by paying particular attention when you are building rapport at the start of the coaching session. Pay attention to the speed, rate, pace, and volume that the person speaks when they are at their most relaxed or at ease. This will give you a good baseline to compare against.

This is useful because it can be telling when people change the speed of their language. So, having a baseline from earlier on gives you a good benchmark for comparison. Often, I find people will slow down when they require more time to think or process things, and that is absolutely fine. You can give them the space and time to do that. They may speed up when they are feeling a little under pressure or stressed, for many different reasons, so it is important to keep your mind open and not make any assumptions. Note the changes. Bring it to the attention of the coachee if you feel that would add value, but before doing so, take note of what they are talking about when the speed changes so that you can be specific with your feedback. (E.g., "I noticed when you speak about person X in your team, you speak more quickly. Tell me about that" or "I noticed when you mentioned your performance review score that you lowered your voice. I could barely hear you. Tell me about that.")

ASK QUESTIONS

We've discussed the importance of asking questions extensively in this book, and I want to remind you again because it is easy to revert to old habits and start giving advice. When your coachee is struggling to find an answer, you may think that you are helping them by offering them an answer. Let me be clear—this is not helpful at all.

I want to remind you of the Belief of Excellence which states that everyone has all the resources they need to resolve all their problems. You must believe this is true of the individuals you coach. When you believe someone is resourceful then they do not need help to find their answers.

I believe that when a coachee doesn't feel resourceful, it is critical that the coach feel resourceful for them. The power of telling someone "I believe in you. I know you can do this" should not be underestimated.

The GROW Coaching Model

The GROW model is without a doubt my preferred format for my coaching sessions. It is easy to follow and easy to explain to the coachee. The model was originally developed in the 1980s by business coaches Graham Alexander, Alan Fine, and Sir John Whitmore. A good way of thinking about the GROW Model is to think about how you would plan a journey. First, you decide where you are going (the goal) and establish where you currently are (your current reality). You then explore various routes (the options) to your destination. In the final step, establishing the will, you ensure that you're committed to making the journey and are prepared for the obstacles that you could encounter on the way.

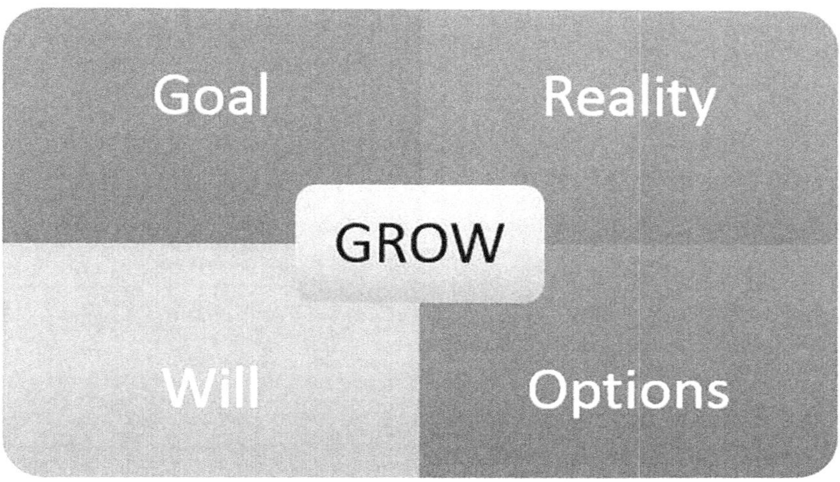

I often find that people think that the model must be followed sequentially—moving from Goal to Reality, to Options, and then Will. The reality is quite different. I often find that a coachee may get clear on the goal, and then move to reality only to conclude that the goal is not really what they want. And that's okay. It's always better to be totally clear on the goal. Otherwise, what is the point?

The advice I give my coaches is to not rush the Goal part of the conversation. I have often spent up to 80% of a 1-hour coaching session just getting clarity on the goal because once the goal is very clear, the other steps of the model come together quickly. If you get the goal wrong at the start, then you are wasting your time and the coachee's time. There is no need to rush through the steps. Be curious about the goal, and the rest will fall into place.

The best way to get a handle on the GROW model is through practice. It lends itself very well to workplace coaching so you can use your team members as guinea pigs. It is particularly useful when used for workplace goals related to an employee's development rather than goals specific to performance (where the employee doesn't have a choice about that particular goal per se).

STEP 1: ELICIT THE GOAL

Once you have set the scene and created rapport you can move to eliciting the goal from your coachee. You can ask as many of the questions below as you need. The questions are not listed in sequence. You can pick the one that works best for you and your coachee.

Sample Goal questions are:

1. What do you want to achieve from this coaching session?
2. What specific goal do you want to achieve?
3. What would you like to happen with _______?
4. What do you want?
5. What would you like to accomplish?
6. What result are you trying to achieve?
7. What outcome would be ideal?
8. What do you want to change?

Even if the coachee is very clear on their goal, I encourage you to keep asking questions. Be curious. You want to make sure that the goal has been thoroughly identified, and the coachee understands their underlying motivations, needs, and expectations.

For example, if you are coaching a team member about their professional development, and they have articulated their goal as "I want to develop my presentation skills so that I can be good at presenting to the executive team," I would then ask questions like:

1. Why are you hoping to achieve this goal?
2. What would the benefits be to you and your career if you reached this goal?
3. What will happen if you do achieve this goal?
4. What will happen if you don't achieve this goal?
5. What would "good" look/sound/feel like?
6. How will you know when you have achieved this goal?
7. Is there anything else important about this goal?
8. If there was another goal that could give you the same benefits and more, what might that goal be?

These questions are used to ensure that the coachee looks at their goal through multiple filters. I have often coached people who choose a professional development goal because they think it's what they should be focusing on rather than taking the time to reflect on what development area would make the most impact on their career and significantly improve their skill set. It is your job as a coach to ensure your coachee has thoroughly thought through all aspects of their goal. This process also serves to increase their motivation and commitment to that goal—which leads me to another important point . . .

When the coachee is talking about the goal, you will want to check for congruence. Is their body language, the tone of voice, energy level, etc. congruent with a goal that this person wants to achieve? If the goal is important to the coachee, you would expect them to communicate in a manner that shows this, whether that be showing excitement, interest, commitment, and even concern or fear (if they believe the goal may be difficult to achieve). If your coachee is showing incongruence in any shape or form, you will want to continue asking questions, and you can also bring the incongruence you see to their attention and ask them to discuss what it might be or represent.

STEP 2: WHAT IS THEIR CURRENT REALITY?

The second step in the GROW model helps you and the employee gain awareness of the current situation. What is going on? What is the particular context? Where are they in relation to the goal? The key is to take this part slow and steady. It does not need to be a rapid-fire interrogation. Give the employee time to think and reflect. Use your active listening skills and remember to maintain rapport. As per the Goal section, you do not have to ask all the questions below. Choose the ones that make the most sense for your coachees' context.

Here are 15 questions designed to clarify their current reality:

1. What is happening now (what, who, when, and how often)?
2. What is the effect or result of this?
3. Have you already taken any steps towards your goal?
4. How would you describe what you did?
5. Where are you now in relation to your goal?
6. On a scale of one to ten, where are you?
7. What has contributed to your success so far?
8. What progress have you made so far?
9. What is working well right now?
10. What is required of you?
11. Why haven't you reached that goal already?
12. What do you think is stopping you?
13. What do you think was happening?
14. Do you know other people who have achieved that goal?
15. What did you learn from _____?

I often find the Reality section uncovers limiting beliefs held by the coachee. When you ask questions like "Have you already taken any steps towards your goal?" or "What do you think is stopping you?" you are likely to get some form of excuse which will link to a limiting belief. For example, I will often hear these kinds of 'excuses':

- I haven't done anything because I haven't had the time.
- I haven't taken any steps because I don't know where to start.
- Nothing is stopping me, but I was waiting for my meeting with you to start.

Always watch out for the use of the words "because" and "but." These are trigger words for you to ask more questions about that particular topic. It is important to shine a light on any limiting beliefs that may hamper the coachee from achieving their goal. The limiting beliefs don't need to be fixed, but they do need to be uncovered and brought to the coachee's attention so that they can be questioned, validated, and addressed.

As a leader, you will often hear "time" being given as an excuse for not getting things done, and often this can be a real issue; however, it still has to be addressed so that it doesn't become a roadblock to the coachee achieving their goal. When I hear "I haven't done anything because I haven't had the time," my next question is "What or who did you prioritize over your goal?" You would want to make sure you have good rapport with the coachee to be this direct, but I like this question because it holds the coachee accountable regarding the use of their time. If someone does not make time for something, it means that there was something else more important or more interesting for them to spend their time on. You will want to know if that behavior is going to change as to achieve the goal.

If you didn't want to be so direct, you could ask a question like "How are you going to make the time to achieve your goal?" or "What will you have to stop spending time on to make time for your goal?"

Similarly, if the coachee were to say to me "I haven't taken any steps because I don't know where to start," my next question would be "If you did know where to start, where might that be?" One of the most useful coaching tools I have learned, and I use it every single day, is the response to "I don't know" from a coachee. When someone says, "I don't know," you respond with "If you did know . . ." I have a 100% success rate with this question. Every single time I ask, "If you did know, what would you do?" the coachee will tell me exactly what they think they should do.

"If you did know . . ." is a compelling question and links back to one of my core beliefs—that everybody knows their answers. I never accept an "I don't know" from anyone, and neither should you. You want to build your coachee's confidence in their ability to solve problems, find answers, set goals, and achieve them. Part of the journey is to ask questions that show that they do have the answers, knowledge, and experience they need to do whatever they want.

STEP 3: WHAT ARE THEIR OPTIONS?

As we move closer to the Will part of the model, the goal starts to become more and more real for the coachee. We're now clear on the goal and the current reality, and it's time to start looking at what options they have open to them for taking action.

Now, you both have a clear understanding of the situation the coaching conversation can proceed to what the employee can do to reach their goal. The option questions you can choose from are:

1. What are your options?
2. What could be your first step?
3. What else could you do?
4. What would happen if you did nothing?
5. What has worked for you already? How could you do more of that?
6. What would happen if you did that?
7. What is the hardest/most challenging part of that for you?
8. What is the best/worst thing about that option?
9. Which option do you feel ready to act on?
10. How have you tackled a similar situation before?
11. What could you do differently?
12. Who do you know who has encountered a similar situation?
13. If anything was possible, what would you do?
14. What else?

In this section of the model, it is critical to elicit as many options from your coachee as possible. This is a great time to remind them that they already have all the resources they need to achieve their goal and you will want them to access all of their internal and external resources. Remember to allow the coachee space to come up with their own options. When you feel like giving advice, ask yourself will this piece of information really help the coachee or is it more about you as a coach needing to participate in the process?

Once the coachee has identified options to move forward and you as a coach observe that the coachee is congruent in relation to those options, you can move forward to the final section of the model.

STEP 4: WHAT IS THE WAY FORWARD?

In this step, you are checking for commitment and helping the employee to establish a clear action plan for the next steps. The outcome of this section is a clear path forward with agreed-upon actions. I always have action starting immediately: "What could you start doing right now, today, to move closer to achieving your goal?" You want to create momentum, and you want to ensure that the coachee is adequately motivated and is committed to taking the necessary action.

I have had coaching sessions where we have got to the Will section, and we identify that the motivation to act is just not there. Achieving a goal without the right levels of motivation is going to be hard, if not impossible. In these situations, we go right back to the Goal section and find a goal that the coachee is motivated to achieve. Don't be disillusioned if this happens because this is the whole purpose of the GROW model—to ensure that the coachee chooses a meaningful goal that they are committed to achieving.

We are all guilty of setting goals for ourselves that aren't important to us and we are not motivated to achieve even when we have the best intentions. It is extremely useful for a coachee to recognize their lack of will or motivation in relation to a specific goal—this can uncover limiting beliefs and oftentimes a recognition that the goal is just not important to them. Remember, it is all about the lesson—there is no such thing as failure only feedback.

Great questions for checking motivation and commitment to the goal are:

1. What will you do first?
2. What do you think you need to do right now?
3. How will you know when you have done it?
4. Is there anything else that you can do?
5. What obstacles could get in the way of success?
6. What resources can help you?
7. Is there anything missing?
8. What step will you take now?
9. When are you going to start?
10. What will happen (or, what is the cost) of you NOT doing this?
11. On a scale of one to ten, how motivated/committed are you to doing it?
12. What would it take to make it a ten?

Again, you are always looking for congruence. When you start to discuss action and getting specific about exactly what measures will be taken, it is common for the coachee to display signs of reticence or worry, and that's okay. It is not okay to ignore those signs. In this situation, I would ask "How could you adapt this action to feel more confident?" or "Do you have any concerns about taking this action?" or "How could you remove any roadblocks?" or "What other resources can you leverage to complete this action with ease?"

I would also recommend using the form we covered earlier, on how to set powerful goals, as means to document the goal in detail, and as a double-check that the will and motivation are indeed there to achieve it. The form on the next page can be used as a reference guide for your first coaching sessions until you get used to the GROW model and its questions.

Summary

Practice makes perfect with the GROW model.

I remember the first time I used the model, I went into the coaching session with a printout of all the questions, and I believe I brought the same piece of paper to my second, third, and fourth coaching sessions. And do you know what? It was fine. By the fifth coaching session, I had certain questions that I found worked well for me as a coach, and I continue to use those questions to this day. Before long, the GROW model just became a part of my coaching conversations—fluid, natural and easy. It will be the same for you.

New coaches tend to get stressed about not knowing the right question to ask at the right time, and if you start worrying about what question you are going to ask your coachee during the coaching session, then you have stopped actively listening and are likely to break rapport. If your attention is on what question you will ask next, then your attention is not where it should be—on your coachee.

Remind yourself of the beliefs of excellence—you have all the resources you need and there is no such thing as failure only feedback. If you are new to coaching, you maybe even notice your own limiting beliefs start to pop up prior to your first coaching session. Use your self-awareness to notice if you are procrastinating and/or finding excuses to delay the coaching—these are all symptoms of underlying limiting beliefs. Here are a couple of the limiting beliefs that came up for me when I first started out:

- I'm not ready
- I don't know enough
- I have to practice more
- I have to study more
- I will let my coachee down
- I won't ask good enough questions.

Conversation with ________________ on ___ /____/ ____

G	Agree What would you like to discuss? What would you like to walk away from this conversation with? If I could grant you a wish for this session, what would it be? What do you want? How will you know when you've got it?	Record agreed-on goals—ensure that they are clear, measurable, and motivating.
R	What is happening at the moment? Where/when/with whom is this happening? What is the effect? What feedback have you received? What does it tell you? What other factors are relevant? What have you tried so far? What is stopping you from . . .?	Briefly describe the consensus you reach or the differences you have.

O	What options do you have? What alternatives are there to that approach? What else could you do? What other approaches have you seen used in similar circumstances? What options do you like most? What are the benefits and pitfalls of these options?	Record what you decide—the options, their ownership, and potential obstacles.
W	What is the first thing you are going to do? When will you do it? What are your next steps? What support do you need? On a scale of 1 to 10, how confident do you feel that you will take these actions? If not 10, what do you need to do to make you more confident?	Briefly record the core aspects of your coaching action plan—transfer to plan.

These limiting beliefs were powerful enough to delay me from coaching team members by weeks and months! I had to remind myself that there was no way that I was going to learn if I didn't take the first step. I took that step, and I haven't stopped since. A close mentor of mine reminded me, back in those days, that there were many people in urgent need of my coaching help and by me delaying and making excuses I was actually denying these people the help that they needed. She also told me that my feeling of being only 50% ready was actually 150% to the coachee that wanted my help.

I have never forgotten that and nor should you.

When you don't feel ready or prepared enough to coach you are denying someone the help that they need AND from their point of view you are more than ready!

And you are.

Workplace Coaching Exercises

CAREER COACHING:
MY CURRENT ROLE

Begin thinking about some of the headlines below. We have given you some questions to guide your thinking. Use a separate sheet of paper if necessary.

Responsibilities/Tasks

In your current role, what are your key responsibilities/tasks? What do you actually do?

1. ....

2. ....

3. ....

4. ....

5. ....

6. ....

7. ....

8. ....

Skills, qualifications, knowledge, and experience

In order to be more effective in your role, what skills, experience, or knowledge do you need to acquire?

1. ....

2. ....

3. ....

4. ....

5. ....

6. ....

7. ....

8. ....

Achievements

Which of your significant achievements are you most proud of, and why?

1. ....

2. ....

3. ....

4. ....

5. ....

6. ....

7. ....

8. ....

Job satisfaction

What do you like most about your current role?

1. ....

2. ....

3. ....

4. ....

5. ....

6. ....

7. ....

8. ....

What do you like least?

1. ....

2. ....

3. ....

4. ....

5. ....

6. ....

7. ....

8. ....

What difficulties do you experience in your role?

1. ....

2. ....

3. ....

4. ....

5. ....

6. ....

7. ....

8. ....

Has this role fulfilled your expectations? If not, why not?

1. ....

2. ....

3. ....

4. ....

5. ....

6. ....

7. ....

8. ....

Summary

Looking through your responses above, what conclusions do you draw? Do any themes appear? Don't worry if there aren't. We will work through some of the other exercises and then come back to this.

1. ....

2. ....

3. ....

4. ....

5. ....

6. ....

7. ....

8. ....

CAREER COACHING:
WHAT MOTIVATES ME AT WORK?

The following exercise will encourage you to think about your own personal work motivators. Read each of the following 35 statements about work values and rate their importance to you based on the following scale.

Transferable Skill		Not Important 1	Of Some Importance 2	Quite Important 3	Important 4	Very Important 5
1	I enjoy having a lot of contact with people.					
2	I enjoy being responsible for work done by others.					
3	I enjoy having lots of different things to do.					
4	I enjoy competing against other people or groups.					
5	I like being able to work in my own way, without being told what to do.					
6	I prefer to choose when to do things, not having rigid working hours.					
7	I would or do like close friendships with people at work.					
8	I enjoy working quickly.					
9	I enjoy being in a position that leads others to respect me.					
10	I like to take risks.					
11	It is important to me to make decisions about how things should be done.					
12	Thinking up new ideas and ways of doing things is important to me.					
13	It is important to me to help other people, either in groups or individually.					
14	Earning a lot of money is important to me.					
15	It is important to me to help other people, either in groups or individually.					
16	I like to work where this is a good chance of promotion.					
17	I enjoy being stretched and given new problems to work on.					
18	I like being part of a well-known organization.					
19	I like a work routine that is fairly predictable.					
20	I like working to deadlines.					
21	I like to live in a place where I can get involved in the community.					
22	I like to work in a team alongside others.					
23	I enjoy doing something that is physically demanding.					
24	I like working on my own.					
25	I enjoy work involving drawing, designing, making things, etc.					
26	I like being able to express ideas well in writing or words.					
27	I like people to look up to me because of what I do.					
28	It is important to know my work will always be there.					
29	It is important that I work in the right part of the country.					
30	I like working at things that involve concentration.					
31	I like to think that my work is producing something worthwhile for society.					
32	I prefer to have few pressures or uncomfortable demands.					
33	I enjoy persuading people to change their minds about something.					
34	It is important to me to learn new things.					
35	I like being known as someone with special knowledge or skills.					

When you have completed the questionnaire, look at each statement that you scored 4 or 5. Which are the most important 5 or 6 of these motivators for you at the moment? Write a summary of these motivators. It will start to paint a comprehensive picture of your key work values and preferences.

My key work motivators are:

....

....

....

....

....

....

....

....

....

....

....

....

In addition, take a moment to think about factors that you have previously been demotivated by. These are things that, when present, make you feel less motivated to exert effort into what you are doing. Write a summary of these demotivation factors. It will further help you build a complete understanding of your preferences.

My key work demotivators are:

....

....

....

....

....

....

....

....

....

....

....

....

How well does your current job satisfy the motivators you have identified? If there isn't a perfect match, you may be able to change this. You may be able to improve the way your present work role meets your motivators, but for some motivators, you may be better off exercising your most important work values.

For example, you may take on a sports coaching role for one of your children's sports teams to fulfill a need for team leadership, or you may take a hobby that satisfies your creative motivators.

When you are ready to change your career or job, assess how well that change will meet your work motivators. Remember also that your values change as you get older, so it can be worthwhile repeating this exercise every few years.

CAREER COACHING:
MY PERSONAL SWOT ANALYSIS

You need to take a look at where you are now using all the information you have available to you from this session. Also, take into account any feedback you have received from either a formal or informal 360 review or from your performance review. Be as open and honest with yourself as possible when you complete this SWOT analysis. It will help you a great deal in understanding where you are and where you want to get to.

Strengths

What am I good at? What do I do better than others? What do others see as my strengths?

…………………………………………………………………………………

…………………………………………………………………………………

…………………………………………………………………………………

…………………………………………………………………………………

…………………………………………………………………………………

Weaknesses

What do I need to improve? What do I avoid? What do I need to face up to?

…………………………………………………………………………………

…………………………………………………………………………………

…………………………………………………………………………………

…………………………………………………………………………………

…………………………………………………………………………………

Opportunities

What could help me to build on my strengths and develop my weaknesses? What opportunities are out there for me?

....

....

....

....

....

....

Threats

What could prevent me from moving forward? Think about blocks, both inside and outside of work, as well as the people and/or situations that could threaten your development. What possible threats do my weaknesses expose me to?

....

....

....

....

....

....

Summary

Thinking more about the exercise you have just completed, summarize the following:

Your top 3 skills/strengths

1. ....
2. ....
3. ....

Your top 3 development areas

1. ....
2. ....
3. ....

Your top 3 opportunities

1. ....
2. ....
3. ....

Your top 3 threats

1. ....
2. ....
3. ....

Now you have identified your strengths and development areas, your opportunities and threats, it may be helpful to look at how these are linked and impact each other. By highlighting these links and their potential implications, you might be able to think of ways to counter their effects or limit their impact.

An example of this is shown below:

I need to improve my presentation skills. (Development area)
There is a presentation skills course coming up next month. (Opportunity)
I may be too busy to attend due to project X. (Threat)
I will ask my manager for support in delivering this project so that I am able to attend. (Proactive action to counter the threat)

CAREER COACHING:
FUTURE VISION

Use a large sheet of paper (perhaps a sheet of flipchart paper) and get creative! Design the future career that you want for yourself and think BIG. There are many stickers, pictures, and magazines that you can use to add to your vision. We encourage you to hang your vision where you can see it, and every time you walk past it, you will be nudged into thinking about the future. And a map of your future plans will begin to emerge. You can always continue to add any ideas as they occur to you.

Think about:

- The skills you will be using
- The people you will be working with (managers, colleagues, customers, clients, and staff)
- How you will be working (employed, self-employed, full time, part-time)
- Will your job involve travel?
- How will this future career really benefit you and those around you (e.g., family)?
- What will this career give you?

It is not about job titles, as there is no guarantee the same jobs or job titles will be around in five years. It is more about what you will be doing, with whom, where, and what the results are. Use the results of the last section to help you with this exercise.

Be realistic. But also remember that you can only choose a direction and aim your efforts towards it. You can never be certain of the opportunities or obstacles you may actually encounter.

When you are done, transfer the results to the summary on the next page.

Summary

The working life I want to lead

1. ....

2. ....

3. ....

4. ....

5. ....

6. ....

The people I'll be working with and how I'll be working with them

....

....

....

....

....

....

How I'll be working (e.g., in an office, frequent travel)

………………………………………………………………………………

………………………………………………………………………………

………………………………………………………………………………

………………………………………………………………………………

………………………………………………………………………………

………………………………………………………………………………

The specialist skills I will have to develop

………………………………………………………………………………

………………………………………………………………………………

………………………………………………………………………………

………………………………………………………………………………

………………………………………………………………………………

………………………………………………………………………………

The value I will be adding to the business

………………………………………………………………………………

………………………………………………………………………………

………………………………………………………………………………

………………………………………………………………………………

………………………………………………………………………………

………………………………………………………………………………

The role models I will represent to colleagues

……………………………………………………………………………………

……………………………………………………………………………………

……………………………………………………………………………………

……………………………………………………………………………………

……………………………………………………………………………………

……………………………………………………………………………………

What people will say about me

……………………………………………………………………………………

……………………………………………………………………………………

……………………………………………………………………………………

……………………………………………………………………………………

……………………………………………………………………………………

……………………………………………………………………………………

Any other points

……………………………………………………………………………………

……………………………………………………………………………………

……………………………………………………………………………………

……………………………………………………………………………………

……………………………………………………………………………………

……………………………………………………………………………………

CAREER DEVELOPMENT:
PERSONAL STRENGTHS EXERCISE

We tend to focus on closing the gap of our perceived weaknesses when the real opportunity for the greatest improvement and growth is to boost our inherent strengths. For example, on a scale of -5 to +5, do you think you would achieve more by shifting weakness from a -3 to a -1, or from boosting a strength from a +3 to a +5? And which would be more enjoyable?

My top 5 strengths are: What qualities do you MOST like about yourself? What are you BEST at? What do you most enjoy?	**I could leverage this strength by:** Review the questions above and identify between three to five actions you can take to fully leverage the strength you have chosen.
	1. 2. 3. 4. 5.
	1. 2. 3. 4. 5.
	1. 2. 3. 4. 5.

	1. 2. 3. 4. 5.
	1. 2. 3. 4. 5.

Write out your top five strengths—those qualities or attributes you possess that give you the most joy and satisfaction. Then for each strength, ask yourself the following questions:

1. How can I turn this strength into an opportunity?
2. How could I use this strength more (potentially in different contexts)?
3. How am I not leveraging this strength to its fullest potential?
4. What is stopping me from being known as someone who exemplifies or models the best of this strength?
5. If I was guaranteed success, what would I do differently to reach my fullest potential with this strength?

Great job!

How does it feel to focus on your strengths? Not too bad, right? Now that you have spent time identifying your key strengths and the opportunities you have to leverage them to the fullest, the next step is to take action.

You might find that there has been some overlap in the actions for each strength. Don't worry. That's a good thing, and we want to make sure that you start to experience the benefits of focusing on your strengths. So, for now, identify the top three actions from the entire list that you want to start taking action on today, and set a date for completion.

Strength	Priority Action	Completion Date
	1.	
	2.	
	3.	

CAREER DEVELOPMENT: CHOOSING YOUR CAREER PATH

Below are twenty questions designed to inspire your thinking concerning your potential career options. The questions are specifically constructed to help uncover patterns of preferences, behavior, and action that may serve to inform your ideal career, and at a very minimum, jog your memory about what you enjoy doing most and why?

We recommend that you take the necessary time to respond to the questions, and the more detail you provide, the better. You probably won't have answered questions like this before, so allow yourself a chance to reflect on your answers and jot down any insights or thoughts that present themselves. You might surprise yourself with what pops up!

What I wanted to be when I grew up:

When you were younger, what did you want to be when you grew up? Consider this from as far back as you can remember. Write down as much detail as you can—however boring, silly or outrageous.

Start with "I remember . . ."

....

....

....

....

....

....

....

....

....

....

....

....

....

....

What specifically attracted you to these careers?

....

....

....

....

....

....

....

....

....

....

Knowing what you know now, which careers—or parts of them—are still:

i) attractive?

………………………………………………………………………………

………………………………………………………………………………

………………………………………………………………………………

………………………………………………………………………………

………………………………………………………………………………

………………………………………………………………………………

………………………………………………………………………………

………………………………………………………………………………

………………………………………………………………………………

………………………………………………………………………………

ii) unattractive?

………………………………………………………………………………

………………………………………………………………………………

………………………………………………………………………………

………………………………………………………………………………

………………………………………………………………………………

………………………………………………………………………………

………………………………………………………………………………

………………………………………………………………………………

………………………………………………………………………………

………………………………………………………………………………

Work Review:

What aspects of these careers, whether good or bad, do you have in your work?

i) currently?

………………………………………………………………………………………

………………………………………………………………………………………

………………………………………………………………………………………

………………………………………………………………………………………

………………………………………………………………………………………

………………………………………………………………………………………

………………………………………………………………………………………

………………………………………………………………………………………

………………………………………………………………………………………

………………………………………………………………………………………

ii) in past roles?

………………………………………………………………………………………

………………………………………………………………………………………

………………………………………………………………………………………

………………………………………………………………………………………

………………………………………………………………………………………

………………………………………………………………………………………

………………………………………………………………………………………

………………………………………………………………………………………

………………………………………………………………………………………

How do you *currently* enjoy yourself at work?

……………………………………………………………………………………

……………………………………………………………………………………

……………………………………………………………………………………

……………………………………………………………………………………

……………………………………………………………………………………

……………………………………………………………………………………

……………………………………………………………………………………

……………………………………………………………………………………

……………………………………………………………………………………

If you won the lottery, became a multi-millionaire, and could choose to be or do *anything*;

i) what would you *be*? What would you *do* with your time?

……………………………………………………………………………

……………………………………………………………………………

……………………………………………………………………………

……………………………………………………………………………

……………………………………………………………………………

……………………………………………………………………………

……………………………………………………………………………

……………………………………………………………………………

ii) What attracts you to these areas above? Answer as fully as you can:

………………………………………………………………………………

………………………………………………………………………………

………………………………………………………………………………

………………………………………………………………………………

………………………………………………………………………………

………………………………………………………………………………

………………………………………………………………………………

………………………………………………………………………………

Hobbies and Interests:

What hobbies or interests have you had in the past (from the earliest to date)?

Start with "I remember . . ."

………………………………………………………………………………

………………………………………………………………………………

………………………………………………………………………………

………………………………………………………………………………

………………………………………………………………………………

………………………………………………………………………………

………………………………………………………………………………

………………………………………………………………………………

What hobbies or interests do you have now?

……………………………………………………………………………

……………………………………………………………………………

……………………………………………………………………………

……………………………………………………………………………

……………………………………………………………………………

……………………………………………………………………………

……………………………………………………………………………

What hobbies or interests would you take up if you had more:

Time?

……………………………………………………………………

……………………………………………………………………

……………………………………………………………………

Money?

……………………………………………………………………

……………………………………………………………………

……………………………………………………………………

Freedom?

……………………………………………………………………

……………………………………………………………………

……………………………………………………………………

What attracts you to these hobbies and interests?

…………………………………………………………………………………

…………………………………………………………………………………

…………………………………………………………………………………

…………………………………………………………………………………

…………………………………………………………………………………

…………………………………………………………………………………

…………………………………………………………………………………

…………………………………………………………………………………

…………………………………………………………………………………

People and Qualities:

Who have you, or do you really love working with?

…………………………………………………………………………………

…………………………………………………………………………………

…………………………………………………………………………………

…………………………………………………………………………………

…………………………………………………………………………………

…………………………………………………………………………………

…………………………………………………………………………………

…………………………………………………………………………………

…………………………………………………………………………………

What qualities do these people have?

……………………………………………………………………………………

……………………………………………………………………………………

……………………………………………………………………………………

……………………………………………………………………………………

……………………………………………………………………………………

……………………………………………………………………………………

……………………………………………………………………………………

……………………………………………………………………………………

……………………………………………………………………………………

……………………………………………………………………………………

Where might you find people with these qualities?

……………………………………………………………………………………

……………………………………………………………………………………

……………………………………………………………………………………

……………………………………………………………………………………

……………………………………………………………………………………

……………………………………………………………………………………

……………………………………………………………………………………

……………………………………………………………………………………

……………………………………………………………………………………

……………………………………………………………………………………

Which of YOUR qualities do you MOST enjoy using?

....

....

....

....

....

....

....

....

....

The Bigger Picture:

So, after reviewing your answers to all the questions above, take some time to answer these final questions:

If there was something you had given up on in your life, what would it be?

....

....

....

....

....

....

....

....

What is your dream?

…………………………………………………………………………………………

…………………………………………………………………………………………

…………………………………………………………………………………………

…………………………………………………………………………………………

…………………………………………………………………………………………

…………………………………………………………………………………………

…………………………………………………………………………………………

…………………………………………………………………………………………

…………………………………………………………………………………………

…………………………………………………………………………………………

What do you want the rest of your life to be about?

…………………………………………………………………………………………

…………………………………………………………………………………………

…………………………………………………………………………………………

…………………………………………………………………………………………

…………………………………………………………………………………………

…………………………………………………………………………………………

…………………………………………………………………………………………

…………………………………………………………………………………………

…………………………………………………………………………………………

…………………………………………………………………………………………

What if there were NO obstacles whatsoever?

....

....

....

....

....

....

....

....

....

....

What do you want to be doing with your life in 10, 15, and 20 years' time?

....

....

....

....

....

....

....

....

....

....

Finally, use the spaces below to review and write the common themes or key pieces of information you have noticed from your answers:

....

....

....

....

....

....

....

CAREER SATISFACTION: OWN YOUR WORK HAPPINESS

The average person will spend 90,000 hours at work over their lifetime. And according to the Quality of Working Life report from the Chartered Management Institute and Workplace Health Connect, 25% of employees say work is their primary source of stress, and 40% say their job is "very or extremely stressful."

Our feelings about our job role can change over time and can range anywhere from abject disillusionment to total delight. Individuals who enjoy their work the most are good at making a distinction between themselves and the results of their work. (E.g., they can detach from how they are measured/perceived at work and their measurement of their self-worth or self-esteem.)

This ability to detach allows for enjoyment of work, independent of circumstances. It's when this distinction isn't made that our happiness or satisfaction becomes dependent on how things are going at work—a risky predicament when many aspects of our jobs are out of the sphere of control. (E.g., redundancies, changes in management, allocation of bonus, promotion decisions, etc.)

To maintain some modicum of balance and control, it is important to identify what you are happy with in your current role and what parts of your job cause you stress or frustration. You may not be able to remove the stressors, but you can become more aware of them and how you can best manage them.

Instructions

The purpose of this exercise is to help you identify three actions you can take to empower yourself in your current work situation. You will also gain some insight into what contributes to how you feel at work by answering the questions below.

Remember to be honest with yourself. Respond to the questions based on your current experiences and feelings, not your desired ones.

What % of your time at work are you feeling:

ENJOYMENT %
IN BETWEEN %
DISCOMFORT %

What would you say most contributes to your enjoyment at work?

....

....

....

....

What would you say most contributes to your discomfort at work?

....

....

....

....

What would you say are the underlying critical elements that affect your enjoyment of your work?

………………………………………………………………………………

………………………………………………………………………………

………………………………………………………………………………

………………………………………………………………………………

………………………………………………………………………………

………………………………………………………………………………

What could you do differently to feel better?

………………………………………………………………………………

………………………………………………………………………………

………………………………………………………………………………

………………………………………………………………………………

………………………………………………………………………………

Now, what will you do differently to empower yourself and take control of your current situation?

Action 1

……………………………………………………………………

……………………………………………………………………

……………………………………………………………………

……………………………………………………………………

Action 2

....

....

....

....

Action 3

....

....

....

....

CAREER DEVELOPMENT: 360 FEEDBACK

One of the benefits of receiving workplace coaching is it improves your self-awareness, and this can be easily done by requesting feedback from your team, your peers, and your manager. Cultivating your self-awareness and understanding how you are perceived by different audiences is critical to your professional development and in ensuring you reach your full potential.

It is normal to have blind spots in terms of our abilities, and this is why titans of business, like Bill Gates (Microsoft) and Eric Schmidt (Google), have publicly stated "everyone needs a coach."

The purpose of this exercise is to enable you to request feedback on your perceived strengths and areas for development. Based on the responses, you can then decide, in conjunction with your coach or manager, the most appropriate action to take.

Step 1: Identify Audience

For this exercise to be truly effective, it is suggested you get a cross section of individuals to provide you with feedback. We recommend the following:

1. Your manager
2. Three colleagues or peers
3. Three team members (if you manage a team)
4. Three cross-functional peers
5. One person with who you do not get on with or regularly experience conflict.

It is also suggested that you choose individuals who will take the necessary time to do this for you properly and will give you honest feedback. So keep in mind your current relationship with these individuals and their likelihood to want to engage in an exercise of this kind.

Note: You may want to suggest that you reciprocate the feedback for them so that it's a win-win.

Step 2: Solicit Feedback

Send this email to the audience you have identified in step one.

Dear (insert person's name),

I am currently working on my learning and development plan. It is important to me to better understand how my colleagues perceive my strengths and weaknesses. I want to be considered a person who is genuinely open to feedback, and I do value your opinion so your honest feedback would be greatly appreciated.

If you would like me to reciprocate with feedback to you, just let me know. I would be more than happy to do this.

The feedback process is very straightforward. I just need your response to the following three questions. The more detail you can provide me, the better.

1. *When you think about me, what comes to mind?*
2. *My Strengths and Talents – what do you value most about me?*
3. *My Weaknesses – how could I be more effective or impactful?*

Thank you in advance for taking the time out of your busy day to give me your feedback.

Kind regards,

(Your name)

Step 3: Analyze Feedback

Once you have received all the responses to your email, take some time to review the responses.

Are there any common themes or patterns?

… …

… …

… …

… …

… …

Are there any surprises, or does it align with how you see yourself?

… …

… …

… …

… …

… …

Describe what specifically you have learned from the feedback.

… …

… …

… …

… …

What most surprised me
was ……………………………………………………………………………

I am most valued
for ……………………………………………………………………………

I could most
improve …………………………………………………………………………

CAREER DEVELOPMENT: BLAST LIMITING BELIEFS

We know that it is important to focus on and leverage our strengths; however, there are times when our perceived weaknesses start to hold us back and have a negative impact on our performance and potential. When this is the case, they need to be addressed and blasted into outer space!

This is a very simple exercise to help you identify your perceived weaknesses and constructively choose a strategy to keep them from holding you back.

Step 1

To start, choose three of the weaknesses that you believe are holding you back the most at work. You may want to ask yourself "What do I most dislike or find most frustrating about myself?" or "How am I stopping myself from reaching my fullest potential?"

Step 2

Then for each weakness ask yourself "How specifically does this get in the way of me achieving my goals or doing my job?"

If you can't identify a specific reason, then this means it is not really a weakness, right? So choose a different weakness that does impact you achieving your goals.

Step 3

Read the Limiting Belief Removal strategies, and then for each weakness, choose one strategy that you are going to use to BLAST that limiting belief. Once you have chosen the strategy, next choose a specific action you are also going to take to ensure this limiting belief is removed and does not return. An example is included below.

Your Four Limiting Belief Removal Strategies

1. **Expectations set too high.** Give yourself a break and stop expecting so much of yourself. Setting the bar too high isn't always a sign of high performance and can often result in quite the opposite. Plus you end up expending a lot of time and energy for minimal gain. Take a step back and consider whether improving in this particular area will really give you the results that you desire. It would also be interesting to consider why you are not yet at the level you want. What is holding you back? If you still feel you need to develop this skill/behavior, be clear and specific on how you will know when you have reached the level you want.
2. **Use all your resources (internal and external).** You have all the resources you need to solve all your problems, AND there is a solution to every problem. Are you leveraging all of your available resources to help you with this weakness? Could you ask for help? Do you know someone who has successfully dealt with a similar issue? Have you asked for advice, done some research, or study? Make sure to use all the resources available to you.

3. **Stand out and be known for something else.** A strategy can be to stand out because of one of your strengths, so much so, that your weakness actually doesn't matter. This goes back again to the fact that leveraging our strengths is a far more successful strategy than developing our weaknesses. What strength could you be known for that would render this weakness irrelevant?
4. **Buddy up!** Find someone who is good at something you are not good at, or really loves doing what you hate doing. Then either learn from them or pay them to do it for you (like outsourcing). The sign of a high performer is the ability to identify a personal weakness and find a creative solution to managing it. Sometimes that means developing some skill in that area, and sometimes it means delegating or outsourcing it.

The 3 weaknesses (or things about myself that) **I dislike the most are:**	**What strategies and actions could I apply here?** Using the four strategies above, come up with at least one strategy and one action for each weakness.
1.	Strategy: Action:
2.	Strategy: Action:
3.	Strategy: Action:

CAREER DEVELOPMENT:
LOVE YOUR LIMITS!

Many of our perceived weaknesses are in fact limiting beliefs that are not based on fact! We often have blind spots about our abilities and our potential. Our inner critic (that little voice in your head) can have a powerful impact on how we view ourselves, AND that voice can sometimes be a horrid little liar! The fact is that many of our perceived weaknesses serve an important purpose in our lives, and when looked at objectively can be viewed as strengths in different contexts.

The Three Weaknesses	**List two (or more) situations where this weakness could be useful or where the weakness serves a purpose.**	
I am not good at planning. I am also impatient and tend to dive in headfirst with new initiatives.	**Situation/Purpose 1** *With initiatives that need to be delivered quickly, this behavior can be seen as a real asset.*	**Situation/Purpose 2** *I have confidence in my abilities, and my team is inspired by my belief in them. My confidence is a good way of modeling my belief that there is no such thing as failure, only feedback.*
	Situation/Purpose 1	**Situation/Purpose 2**
	Situation/Purpose 1	**Situation/Purpose 2**
	Situation/Purpose 1	**Situation/Purpose 2**

This exercise helps you reframe the limiting beliefs you hold about yourself and will give you a new perspective on their purpose and value. Simply answer the questions above and see where your weaknesses are also strengths.

What have you learned about yourself from doing this exercise?

... ...

... ...

... ...

... ...

... ...

... ...

... ...

CAREER DEVELOPMENT:
STOP, START, CONTINUE

The Stop Start Continue Change management model is a well-known, tried and tested model used by organizations looking to make improvements of all types (e.g., service improvements, process improvements, performance improvements, people improvements). The model is deceptively simple and highly effective.

In this context, we will use it to look at your performance and identify behaviors and activities that you would want to stop, start, or continue to reach your goals.

START: To achieve your goals, what do you want to start doing? Make a list of ideas/items that you are not doing yet, but you should be; new ideas that you have thought of or have not been considered before, and maybe feedback that you have received from your manager or colleagues that would enhance your performance.

STOP: To achieve your goals, what should you stop doing? Make a list of ideas/items that are not working for you or your team; are not having the desired outcome; things that you just dislike and are not working for you.

CONTINUE: To achieve your goals, what should you continue doing? Make a list of ideas/items that are working well for you and you are happy with the results; that your team or manager likes, and thinks are successful.

STOP	START	CONTINUE

GOAL SETTING & PLANNING:
START THE YEAR STRONG

Your goals must be:

Measurable. You need to be able to measure your progress.

Specific. You need to be able to answer the question "What exactly do you want?"

Time-bound. You need to know when you will start and when you will finish.

Natural. It has to be aligned with who you are and your talents, passion, and skills.

Understandable. Make it simple and put it in simple words.

Enthusiastic. It has to put a smile on your face when you imagine reaching it.

Realistic. Dream, and get out of your comfort zone, keeping in mind that you are planning one year, not your whole life.

STEPS TO CREATE AN EFFECTIVE GOAL

Step 1: Evaluate the previous year

What did you achieve last year? Right down everything you can think of, no matter how small.

1. ....
2. ....
3. ....
4. ....
5. ....
6. ....
7. ....
8. ....
9. ....
10. ....
11. ....
12. ....
13. ....
14. ....
15. ....

What did you like about last year, habits that you want to keep in this coming year?

1. ....

2. ....

3. ....

4. ....

5. ....

6. ....

7. ....

8. ....

9. ....

10. ....

What didn't you like about last year, habits that you want to get rid of in the coming year?

1. ....

2. ....

3. ....

4. ....

5. ....

6. ....

7. ....

8. ....

9. ....

10. ....

Step 2: Set Your Goals

Write down twenty goals that you want to accomplish.

- Things you want to BE
- Things you want to HAVE
- Things you want to DO

1. ....

2. ....

3. ....

4. ....

5. ....

6. ....

7. ....

8. ....

9. ....

10. ....

11. ....

12. ....

13. ....

14. ....

15. ....

16. ....

17. ....

18. ....

19. ....

20. ....

Make sure to put goals in all areas of your life including Spiritual goals, self-growth, health & fitness, love and family, social life, career & finance.

After finishing step two, put a number beside each goal. The number indicates the number of years it will take you to reach this goal. Choose the top 3–5 goals that can be accomplished in one year in each area of life, and write them in the next step.

Step 3: Get Balance

My top 3–5 goals are:

1. ....

2. ....

3. ....

4. ....

5. ....

In case your goals don't cover all these aspects, make sure to add some goals to have a balanced life.

1. Spiritual life
2. Self-Growth
3. Health & Fitness
4. Love & Family
5. Social life
6. Career
7. Finance

1. ....

2. ....

3. ....

Step 4: Get Committed

Now that you know what you want to accomplish next year and you have balanced goals, you need to write one paragraph on each goal, explaining why you want to do it and what will happen if you don't. If you cannot write down one paragraph easily, this goal is not that important to you. You need to have enough reasons to do it. I suggest you use some sheets of paper to write these down.

... ...

... ...

... ...

... ...

... ...

... ...

... ...

... ...

... ...

... ...

When planning for success, it is important to think about what obstacles you might face while reaching your goal? How are you going to overcome them? If you are truly passionate about reaching this goal, you will find a way.

Goal	Obstacle	Plan to Overcome

Step 5: Take Action Now

Ask yourself "What can I do right now to start working on my goals?" Take action, no matter how small it is. You must take an action on each goal. It might be a phone call, sharing some ideas with family, or asking for support.

What decision do I have to make right now to take a step closer to my goals?

Goals	**What can I do right now?**	**What decision do I have to make?**

Step 6: Be Smart

Use all your available resources. What internal and external resources can you access or leverage in order to increase your chance of achieving your goals?

1. ....

2. ....

3. ....

4. ....

Who can help me achieve my goal or give me any kind of support? Make a support network for each goal and know who you can share your goal with.

Get the Right Education

List of books I want to read to get closer to my goals

1. ....

2. ....

3. ....

4. ....

List of courses and/or seminars I want to attend to be able to reach my goals

1. ....

2. ....

3. ....

4. ....

Get a Coach

One of the best tools to reach your goals is to hire a coach. A coach will help you get from where you are to where you want to be and can make your journey more exciting.

Step 7: Plan Your Year

It's time to make a detailed plan for the next twelve months. Write down each goal. Beside it, write down the expected start date and end date, then list the steps you will take to reach the desired outcome.

Goal	Start Date	End Date	Steps
			1. 2. 3.
			1. 2. 3.
			1. 2. 3.
			1. 2. 3.
			1. 2. 3.
			1. 2. 3.

Goal	Start Date	End Date	Steps
			1. 2. 3.
			1. 2. 3.

CAREER DEVELOPMENT: VALUES

What are values?

- Values are abstract concepts.
- Values are what are important to us. They motivate us.
- They are also criteria for determining whether our actions are right or wrong.
- They determine how we spend our time.
- They may be different in different contexts.
- They are related to beliefs and each other.
- They are in a hierarchy. Some are more important than others.

This is a fun exercise, and it really helps people uncover the values that drive their motivations and ultimately their behavior. For this specific exercise, we are going to use the context of the coaches' careers (i.e., uncover their values specific to their careers).

Ask the coachee to look through the list of values and choose the 10 values that resonate with them the most in relation to what is important to them about their career. They are only allowed to choose 10. Once they have chosen the 10, ask them to remove 5 of the values they have chosen. Once they have done that, ask them to remove three more and then two more so that they are left with just one value. You should hear your coachee groan through this exercise, and that's good because it should be difficult for them to remove their values.

On completion of the exercise, you can ask them if they found the exercise easy or hard (most people will say very hard). You can ask them why it was hard. You can ask, "Are you surprised at the values you removed from the list?" An important point here is that people put their own meaning on their values (i.e., two people may choose "family" as their most important value, but "family" may mean very different things to each person). So ask your coachee what their value means to them. Then ask how this value can be met for them in relation to their career. This helps give the coachee important insight into what they should be looking for when choosing a career and/or making decisions about career changes, promotions, etc.

A key lesson from this exercise is that we all have values that drive our behavior, and these values are very deeply held. It is important to understand that we are all motivated by different values and these values can be seen at work.

Values	**Values**
Acceptance	Intuition
Achievement	Joy
Acknowledgment	Justice
Adventure	Kindness
Affection	Knowledge
Amazement	Leadership
Ambition	Learning
Amusement	Longevity
Appreciation	Love
Approval	Loyalty
Assertiveness	Making a difference
Attractiveness	Mastery
Balance	Meaning
Beauty	Mindfulness
Being the best	Motivation
Belonging	Mysteriousness
Bravery	Nature

Values	Values
Brilliance	Non-conformity
Capability	Open-mindedness
Care	Optimism
Challenge	Order
Change	Organization
Comfort	Outdoors
Commitment	Patience
Community	Passion
Confidence	Peace
Connection	Perseverance
Consistency	Persuasiveness
Control	Playfulness
Cooperation	Pleasure
Correctness	Popularity
Country	Power
Courage	Presence
Creativity	Pride
Credibility	Professionalism
Curiosity	Prosperity
Decisiveness	Recognition
Delight	Reliability
Dependability	Religiousness
Dignity	Reputation
Discipline	Respect
Discovery	Responsibility
Diversity	Sacrifice
Dreaming	Security
Education	Self-control
Effectiveness	Self-respect
Efficiency	Service

Values	**Values**
Empathy	Significance
Encouragement	Simplicity
Endurance	Sincerity
Energy	Solitude
Enjoyment	Speed
Excellence	Spirit
Exploration	Status
Fairness	Strength
Faith	Success
Family	Support
Fearlessness	Surprise
Financial independence	Sympathy
Fitness	Teaching
Focus	Teamwork
Freedom	Thankfulness
Friendliness	Tranquility
Fun	Trust
Generosity	Truth
Gratitude	Uniqueness
Growth	Unity
Guidance	Usefulness
Happiness	Variety
Harmony	Victory
Health	Vision
Honesty	Vitality
Humility	Warmth
Humor	Wealth
Impact	Winning
Independence	Wisdom

GAINING PERSPECTIVE: PERCEPTUAL POSITIONS

Success in the workplace is often based on creating and maintaining successful relationships with your manager, your team, and your colleagues. That can sometimes be hard to do because we don't always see eye-to-eye; however, your ability to see beyond your needs and expectations will be critical to your long-term success. The most successful leaders and entrepreneurs can step into other people's shoes to better understand their points of view. When you want to close a big deal, or gain support for your new idea, it is critical that you step into the roles of your audience. Walk in their shoes to gain perspective and insight into their desires. This allows the individual to cultivate win-win scenarios because not only are they clear on what they want for themselves, they are also clear on what their intended audience wants too. This ability can be used in multiple contexts: negotiating deals, presenting to senior executives, managing your team, dealing with conflict, etc.

You can look at any interaction with a person from three distinct viewpoints. These are most commonly known as perceptual positions.

Position 1: This is your viewpoint.
Position 2: This is the other person's viewpoint.
Position 3: This is the view of an observer.

Now Position 1 is obviously the easiest for any of us to access because it's how we feel, think, experience the world around us, and what we want. In this position, we are most concerned about ourselves, our needs, our agenda, our viewpoints, etc.

Position 2, on the other hand, involves you putting yourself in the other person's shoes. When you take this position, you can begin to understand how the other person feels, what they might be thinking, what is important to them, what they might want, why they are behaving in a certain way, etc. This is valuable information that cannot be accessed if you only remain in Position 1.

Finally, Position 3—the observer. This position allows you to step back and take an objective view of a particular situation. From this position, you can observe the behaviors and interactions of the individuals in Positions 1 and 2. From here, you can detach from the emotions of a situation and look quite dispassionately at the facts of a situation. Taking Position 3 is particularly useful when conflict situations arise, or you feel your emotions are too high to deal objectively with a person or in a given context.

The Pros and Cons

There are pros and cons to each of the perceptual positions. I think you will agree that we spend most of our time in Position 1; however, that can lead to being perceived as selfish or only working in your own self-interest. In contrast, if you are a people pleaser and spend very little time in Position 1, but you are more often in Position 2 then you risk not looking after your own interests enough, and you could be perceived as a pushover or doormat.

If you spend too much time in Position 3, you risk being too detached from people and situations, and you may be perceived as having no feelings or being a cold fish. While objectivity is important, it is also important to be in touch with your own feelings and the feelings of others.

Flexibility is the key here. The ability to move between these positions when the time is right will help you gain important perspective, insight, and understanding of yourself and others.

Exercise

Take a moment to think of a real situation that you have at work where you could benefit from understanding another person's perspective. This may be someone you regularly are in conflict with, but not necessarily so. It could also be a situation where you would benefit from taking a different point of view or understanding someone else's perspective.

Steps

If you choose to, you can do this exercise with your eyes closed or open. It is totally up to you.

1. Think about a relationship at work that you would like to improve or an individual whose perspective you would like to gain.
2. Put yourself into Position 1, and imagine the other person is here right now and that you are looking at him/her. Describe the other person and your feelings about them.
3. Now imagine you are in the other person's shoes, looking at yourself in Position 1. Assume the perspective, beliefs, and assumptions of the other person as if you were that person for a moment. From this perspective, describe the "you" that is in Position 1 and your feelings about the person, using that person's language when you refer to the Position 1 "you."
4. Now step into the observer position—Position 3—and view the relationship between yourself and the other person. Keep in mind what you experienced about the perspective and points of view of both yourself and the other person. To gain total objectivity as the observer, pretend you do not know either of the individuals in Positions 1 and 2. What are your insights into the interaction between the individuals in Positions 1 and 2?

What insights have you gained from this exercise?

……………………………………………………………………………………

……………………………………………………………………………………

……………………………………………………………………………………

……………………………………………………………………………………

……………………………………………………………………………………

……………………………………………………………………………………

……………………………………………………………………………………

……………………………………………………………………………………

What action(s) are you going to take based on your insights?

… …

… …

… …

… …

… …

… …

… …

… …

Printed in Great Britain
by Amazon

17956531R00139